# The Power of the Shade

Jacqueline Wilson

# THE POWER

## OF THE

# SHADE

Oxford University Press 1987
*Oxford Toronto Melbourne*

Oxford University Press, Walton Street,
Oxford OX2 6DP

Oxford New York Toronto
Delhi Bombay Calcutta Madras Karachi
Petaling Jaya Singapore Hong Kong Tokyo
Nairobi Dar es Salaam Cape Town
Melbourne Auckland

and associated companies in
Beirut Berlin Ibadan Nicosia

Oxford is a trade mark of Oxford University Press

British Library Cataloguing in Publication Data

Wilson, Jacqueline
The power of the shade.
I. Title
823'.914 [F]   PZ7

ISBN 0-19-271568-2

Set by Leaper & Gard Ltd, Bristol, England

Printed in Great Britain
by Biddles Ltd, Guildford

This is Emma's book —
and it's also for Teresa, Kylie
and Victoria

# Chapter 1

I am a witch.

It sounds so stupid. Of course it's all nonsense. I don't believe a word of it. Yet I can still feel the soft surprising touch of Selina's lips on mine. It is as if she's left a little part of herself with me. Her lips have shaped mine and so my words are coming out differently now. Has she cast a spell? Perhaps I shall soon start spitting diamonds, spewing toads.

I've suspected Selina of many things but never witchcraft — although I've certainly known she can charm and she can curse. I've always been scared of her. I couldn't believe it when she made friends with me last summer. When we went back to school in September I expected her to start teasing and tormenting me all over again, but she still seemed to like me. We whispered in lessons and walked round the playground with linked arms. I didn't see much of her out of school but that wasn't surprising given our circumstances.

I didn't see her over Christmas. She had gone to France with her family and when she came back she seemed busy with her boyfriend. The Sunday before we went back to school she phoned me up and asked me to come over for the afternoon. I knew she wanted to copy all the holiday homework from me. I resented this. I even considered leaving my schoolbag at home and telling Selina to do her own donkeywork. I only considered it. I ended up the donkey.

But Selina seemed so pleased to see me that I cheered

7

up. I felt stupidly shy of her when she opened the door. She looked at least eighteen in her new black dress. She wore some strange dark red beads round her white neck and she'd tied her long hair up at one side with a red chiffon scarf. She hugged me unselfconsciously and I smelt her expensive jasmine scent. She seemed prepared for a party and for a moment I was terrified. It was a great relief to find we had the house entirely to ourselves.

I thought we'd go up to Selina's bedroom but she led me into the beautiful white living room as if I was a grown-up guest. She had a record playing, melancholy violin music, not Selina's usual top twenty taste at all. She sat on the white leather sofa and waved her hand at the coffee table.

'I thought you might like some supper,' she said.

It wasn't the usual schoolgirl snacks, coke and crisps and bars of chocolate. Selina had a bottle of sparkling white wine still misty from the fridge and a festive cake on a white fluted plate. I had never drunk wine before. The only alcohol I'd ever tried was a sip of Grandad's Guinness, and I found that disgusting. The wine was reassuringly sweet and I felt sophisticated sipping it while I ate my cake. I had had a surfeit of stale chocolate log at teatime but Selina's cake was wondrously different. It was a ring of sweet soft syrupy pastry, rich with peel and candied fruit.

'This is the most delicious cake I've ever had,' I said, surreptitiously wiping the syrup from my plate with my finger.

'Have another slice,' said Selina, helping me. 'It's a special cake for Twelfth Night called a Gateau des Rois.'

I had helped Nan and Auntie Win unwind the fairy lights and tinsel and trinkets from our ugly everlasting tree this morning. I had no idea Twelfth Night could be celebrated in more stylish fashion.

'Watch out for a little hard bit,' said Selina, as I bit into my second slice. 'It'll be a bean.'

I blinked at her.

8

'A dried broad bean. They put one in each cake and then whoever gets it in their slice is supposed to be the king or queen for the evening.'

I sifted the delicious mixture through my teeth but Selina found the bean in her own slice.

'I'm the Queen!' she said, sticking out her tongue with the bean neatly poised on its tip. 'I'm supposed to have a proper gold paper crown, only I haven't got one. Never mind, I'll use my beads.'

She said her mother had given her the string of antique amber beads for her Christmas present. She unfastened her necklace and threaded it through her hair. The rich red beads glowed against the glossy black and made a very passable jewelled crown.

'Now I am the Queen you will have to be my loyal subject,' said Selina.

'That's the game we always play,' I said.

Selina laughed. She poured us both another glass of wine and I sat and showed her all my holiday home-work answers. I even let her copy a couple of my essays almost word for word. She wrote quickly and efficiently in her beautiful italic handwriting. My scrawled pages looked like the hasty counterfeits. I felt depressed and drained my wine. It had an unnerving effect. My head felt only loosely attached to my neck, as if it might spin round of its own accord. I tilted it experimentally and Selina frowned at me. I blushed and went on blushing all over my body, burning in that ice white living room. I sat on the edge of the white leather sofa as if I was in danger of scorching it. I sat so far on the edge that when I rummaged in my shabby schoolbag for another book I lost my balance and slid onto the carpet, banging my bottom.

'Oh May, you are a fool,' said Selina. 'You're not drunk, are you?'

'Of course I'm not,' I said, but my tongue seemed to swell and my voice slurred.

'Two tiddly little glasses!' Selina mocked. 'Here, finish up the cake. It'll help you sober up a bit. I need

9

you to tell me what happened in *Pride and Prejudice* and that French Revolution book.'

I ate the cake but it made me feel odder than ever. I had read *Pride and Prejudice* twice but now I had difficulty recalling the plot. Selina grew tired of listening.

'Yeah, yeah, I think I've got it now,' she said when I was only halfway through. 'I've seen it on the telly anyway. So. *The Time of the Terror*. What's it like? Boring?'

'Very. And it's disgusting too. The tortures!'

'Oh well. It sounds a bit livelier than those soppy Bennett sisters.'

'It isn't, Selina, it's awful. I don't know what this Robert Campbell is going to be like.'

'Is there a photo of him on the cover?' Selina peered over my shoulder. 'No. Pity. Here, he's written an awful lot. He must have been around ages. Oh God, there's this other book that's set in the Thirties. You don't think he was actually around then, do you? He'll be positively senile.'

'And sinister. The tortures go on page after page. It's all about the Queen's friend, the Princesse de Lamballe, and the things that they *do* to her.' I shuddered and the wine and rich cakes inside me slid uneasily from side to side in my stomach.

'Find me the bit,' said Selina eagerly.

'No. It's making me feel sick.'

'Oh, you precious petal, you. I love a good gory bit of torture.' Selina's eyes were shining.

'This book isn't fun. You don't understand, Selina. They cut off her breasts. And then, it's so awful, they tear her apart —'

'Oh that's nothing compared with some of the tortures in the witch trials,' said Selina. 'My mother's got this book and it is incredible the things they did. It was often to girls our age or even younger. There were these huge witch hunts and they tortured them for weeks and then burnt them at the stake. They strangled them first if they confessed. Which I suppose is better

10

than being burnt alive. I'd confess.'

And then she said it.

'Shall I confess to you, May? You'll never guess what. I'm a witch.'

I didn't even take it in at first. My head felt as if all the sticky syrupy cake was stuffed inside it. And then when I realised what she'd said I thought she was joking. She started talking about white witches and black witches and the occult arts and I thought she was making it all up, playing another game.

'I was initiated the day I started my period,' she said. 'My mother performed this special secret ceremony. I swore never to tell a soul. Only I've told you now, haven't I, May? So I'm in danger of my tongue being torn out by the root. Oh dear, oh dear.' She waggled her pretty pink tongue at me mockingly. 'What would I do then, mm?'

'You'd have to cast a magic spell to make it grow again,' I said hoarsely, hoping I'd adopted the right tone. I was so thirsty that I licked up the last drops of wine in my glass.

'God, you're turning into a right lush now,' said Selina. 'Here, have a proper glass full.'

'No, really, I —'

'Shut up,' said Selina, pouring. She sipped from her own glass. 'You can't cast spells whenever you feel inclined. It doesn't work like that. You have to invoke the right energy. It's exhausting, using up all that psychic power. You should see my mother sometimes, she can barely *move*.'

I glanced at her suspiciously. I still thought she was teasing me.

'After a heavy session down the Coven?' I said. 'I suppose all that cauldron stirring must make your arm ache.'

Selina sighed.

'You don't believe me, do you?'

'Of course I don't.'

She stretched and slid elegantly off the sofa. She

11

turned the record over and more violin music filled the room, soft and sad and very strange. She stood in front of me, her eyes dark enigmatic slits. She was staring at me. The stare went on for ever. I stared back and I went on staring even when the white room seemed to spin around us in a whirl of light. I seemed to be whirling too, and I wanted to shut my eyes and cling to the sofa but I went on staring and Selina went on staring until at last she smiled.

'I can make you a witch if you want,' she whispered.

'How?' I croaked like a frog.

'I can initiate you. I'm really supposed to, I don't have the full power, and my mother would go spare if she knew — but she won't know, will she? We won't tell.'

'What–what do I have to do?'

'It's all right. We'll keep it simple,' said Selina, smiling at a secret joke. 'Of course we should really be sky-clad.'

'What?'

'How do you feel about taking your clothes off?'

My heart started thudding.

'Don't look so terrified,' said Selina scornfully. 'Now, we *do* need a pentacle.'

'A what?'

'A star shape with five points. Other witches use a circle, but we practise the Craft in our own special way.'

Selina paced the room and stopped in front of the Christmas tree. It was an elaborate silver affair festooned with glass bells and baubles. She unwound a long length of tinsel and spread it out carefully in the middle of the white carpet in the shape of a star. She kicked off her shoes and stepped inside. Then she beckoned me. I walked over to her, grinning stupidly. I nearly overbalanced again as I bent to undo my shoes. But when I stepped into the pentacle with Selina I stopped feeling self conscious. It was as if I'd stepped into a different state of consciousness altogether. Selina stood so close to me that our breasts gently touched.

She held her hands up and pressed her cool palms against mine, looking deep into my eyes.

'By birth and by secret initiation I am a daughter of the great Moon Goddess,' she whispered, her sweet wine breath tickling my face. 'I have her fey and fecund blood in my veins. I pray to her holy sphere in the sky and she shines down on me and sighs in my soul. She has waxed and waned since the world began and throughout the dance of time her daughters have worshipped her and appropriated her luminous power. It is the power of the light and the power of the shade. The powers suffuse my spirit. They surge and sear my body. I call the powers to my lips and fingertips. Touch my fingertips. Touch my lips. Take the powers. Take them into your own body, your own spirit. Be a vessel for the power of the light and the power of the shade.'

Her palms pressed. Her lips lightly brushed mine. My whole body started tingling. Selina's eyes were so close they seemed to merge into one dark shining orb.

Then she drew away and stepped out of the small pentacle. I was left inside it alone.

'Say "I commend my soul to the Great Goddess of the Night Sky. I desire the power of the light and the power of the shade".'

I mumbled it, in such a state I could barely remember the words.

'Again. You have to say it seven times,' Selina commanded.

So I said it over and over, losing count, but Selina was counting for me, and when I was finished she took hold of me by the shoulders and spun me round and round inside the pentacle. I spun until I staggered, but Selina caught my hand and helped me step out, back onto ordinary white carpet.

She smiled at me, keeping hold of my hand.

'Hello, sister,' she said softly. 'Now you are a witch too.'

# Chapter 2

'I'd like to introduce you to Mr Campbell, girls.' Miss Beecham smiles at him, smiles at us, one big smile, but she seems distracted. Mr Campbell has come as a bit of a shock. He isn't old for a start. I'm not any good at guessing men's ages. Twenty something? He's got very short fluffy dark hair and dark eyes behind big red plastic glasses. A matching scarlet heart is knitted into his black sweater. His jeans are very tight but he's thin enough for it to look okay. He doesn't look a bit like a writer in spite of his glasses. All the girls are whispering and nudging each other and sitting up straight. Especially Selina.

She sits right at the front now, so that Miss Beecham can 'keep an eye' on her. Selina is the most disruptive girl in our form and works hard at building her reputation. She's also the prettiest. She looks particularly striking today because she's experimenting with a new hairstyle. All girls with long hair are supposed to tie it back neatly in a plait or ponytail but most of the teachers have given up nagging at Selina. I'm the only other girl with long hair in our form. Nan still scrapes mine back into a fat red pigtail and ties it with a green ribbon. You'd think I was four years old, not fourteen. Whereas Selina looks years older. She's piled half her long black hair onto the top of her head and secured it with a pink paperclip slide and several pearlised pins. She looks Japanese with her geisha white face and dark almond eyes. She's looking at Mr Campbell. And he's looking at her.

I'm sick of Selina. Why does it always have to be her? Why can't he look at me?

'We're very lucky to have our very own Writer-in-Residence this year,' Miss Beecham burbles. 'I know 4a are particularly looking forward to working with you, Mr Campbell. They're our top stream. They will all be taking nine or ten GCSE's next year, and some of them are actually very gifted at English.'

Mr Campbell murmurs politely. There's not much else he can do.

'I thought it would be particularly useful if 4a studied *Time of the Terror*,' she says. 'They're going to be covering the French revolution in their History syllabus and there's going to be a school trip to Paris next term so it seemed an ideal choice. I managed to get hold of 30 copies just before the end of term, and every girl read it during the Christmas holidays. That's right, isn't it, girls?'

She waits for positive response. Mr Campbell looks puzzled.

'And I'm sure you all enjoyed it as much as I did. Didn't you, girls?' Miss Beecham prompts heavily.

We nod and murmur although I know most of them haven't even got past chapter one.

'*Time of the Terror*?' says Mr Campbell.

He looks so bewildered that Miss Beecham waves a copy of his book at him. He takes it from her and flicks through it.

'Oh dear,' he says. 'I'd better be honest. I haven't actually read it myself.'

Miss Beecham titters uneasily, thinking he's joking.

'I'd like you to know that I gave a copy to Miss Dellmore, our Head of History, and she was very impressed by the historical detail. She couldn't fault you at all, although she tried her hardest.' She smiles to show she's having a go at a joke too.

'I'm afraid there's been a bit of a mix-up,' says Mr Campbell. 'I didn't write this. I'm *Robin* Campbell, not Robert Campbell.'

15

Miss Beecham sways with the shock.

'You didn't write *Time of the Terror?*'

'Sorry.'

'But I don't understand. I arranged it all with the Arts Association. I explained that we particularly wanted a children's writer and —'

'I do write children's books.'

'Oh. I see. What–what name do you write under?'

'Robin Campbell,' Robin Campbell says patiently.

'And what sort of children's books do you write?'

'Modern ones. Here.' He opens his battered brief-case, hunts through a whole pile of books, and finds a paperback. The cover is bent back and the pages are dog-eared. 'This is one of mine.'

His hand is trembling slightly although he doesn't look at all nervous. It makes me like him a lot more.

Miss Beecham looks at his book worriedly. 'I see. Yes. Oh yes, I think I've read about this one in the T.E.S. Isn't it the one where the boy ...? I'm not sure that —' In her agitation Miss Beecham starts rolling up the long floppy bow of her blouse. She looks as if she'd like to roll herself into a tight little ball too. 'Perhaps — as the girls have done all this work and the fifth and lower sixth have read Mr Campbell's Tudor and Stuart books — perhaps I ought to get in touch with *Robert* Campbell?'

'Well actually, I think he's dead now,' says this Mr Campbell.

Selina bursts out laughing and Miss Beecham glares at her.

'Oh dear. This is all so embarrassing. You see, although I'm sure your work is very highly thought of, it might be a bit *too* modern for us, if you see what I mean. It is a church school. Some of the governors might —'

'Well, your school governors have actually appointed me as a Writer-in-Residence up until July. Appointed and paid hard cash. So it looks as if I'm here whether you want me or not.'

'Oh! Well, of course we want you. I didn't mean ...
We're very lucky to have you. It was just — it's a shame
that we can't go ahead with this special French history
project. Never mind. If you give me the titles of all your
books, Mr Campbell, I'll see what I can do about getting copies — although I think we've used up this year's
book fund now. Oh dear. Meanwhile, perhaps you'd
like to tell us about them?'

'I've written five teenage novels. This is the latest.' He
taps the tattered paperback. 'It's written in diary form,
supposedly by a boy of thirteen.'

'Here, is it *Adrian Mole*?' Louise asks eagerly.

'No it isn't. I wish it was in a way — then I'd be rich.
I expect a lot of you have read *Adrian Mole*? I brought a
copy of it with me, and some other funny fictional
diaries. Has anyone read *Diary of a Nobody*? Oh well, I
must read you a bit. And then I've got some real diaries
too, Anne Frank's diary, Kilvert, even an extract from
old Sam Pepys.' He smiles at Miss Beecham. 'A bit of
History after all.'

She smiles back uncertainly, but motions to him to
take the teacher's chair at the front of the class. She sits
on top of an empty desk by the door, her grey Goray
skirt riding up over her plump knees. She swings her
legs every now and then to emphasise her casual pose.
Now that so many of the staff are in their early twenties
the old teachers like Miss Beecham try too hard to be
modern. Her legs are alarmingly apart. I bet Robin
Campbell can see her knickers. I don't think they will
inflame him. Depressing Damart thermals, without a
doubt. I wonder what Robin Campbell wears? Little
black briefs, very chic.

I look at his jeans, seeing if I can spot any line, and
he looks up from *The Diary of a Nobody*, straight at me.
Oh God. My face bursts into flame. I bend my head,
my heart thumping. I think of snow, frost, glaciers but
my body still burns in the tropics.

He reads aloud well. He gives Mr Pooter a genteel
London accent, a Victorian version of Arthur Daley that

17

gets everyone laughing. He laughs once or twice too, almost too sure of himself. Yet when I dare look at him again his hands are still trembling. I wonder if Selina has noticed. She's staring at him intently. The sort of stare that seems to last for ever. The stare that bewitched me.

I still don't know if it was all an elaborate game yesterday. I went home in a daze. I was too excited to sleep, still fancying myself inside the silver pentacle with Selina — but this morning it all seemed so odd and unlikely that I started wondering if I'd dreamt it.

I couldn't wait to see Selina at school. She waved at me casually across the classroom and started chatting about some pop programme on the television last night as if the afternoon in her weird white living room had never happened. I looked at her lips as she talked and tried to imagine them chanting secret charms and then closing over mine. Just thinking it made me blush. So had I imagined the whole thing? No, that was ridiculous, I had gone to Selina's house, I'd eaten the cake and drunk the wine, I still had a headache because I had drunk too much.

'Selina, you know yesterday? The pentacle and —'

'Shut up,' she snapped, and then she carried on about the television programme as if I hadn't even spoken.

I thought it was because Louise and Carol and some of the others were sitting near us and might be listening. I waited until Selina and I were alone together in the cloakrooms after prayers.

'Am I really a witch?' I whispered.

Selina stared past me at her own reflection in the looking glass. She played with the pins in her hair. She didn't say anything. She smiled at herself approvingly.

'Are you a witch?' I persisted.

Selina caught a stray lock of hair and skewered it into place.

'You are a fool, May,' she said, skewering me into my place too.

18

I stare at her now, wondering if I'll ever find out. And she stares at Mr Campbell. I draw eyes on my jotter, a whole series of eyes, staring, staring, staring.

Miss Beecham tiptoes out halfway through the session. It makes a difference. Robin Campbell stops reading out of the different diaries (he hasn't read from his own book yet. I wish he would. I want to see what it's like) and starts talking to us.

'Who's ever kept a diary themselves?'

I've tried.

My mother kept a diary throughout her schooldays. She started when she was six, carefully printing: 'I painted a picter of some pritty flowers. I got a star at school. Aunty gave me a toffee' in a little Letts schoolgirl diary. Nan and Grandad started giving me the diaries, one each year every Christmas, and they used to give me a new empty diary too. They did this right up until last year, even though my own diaries usually petered out by the end of January. My mother never missed a single day. The diaries are dense with her writing, and the later ones are illustrated too, all flowers and frilly frocks and funny little people.

So last year I tried doing little pencil portraits on every page but they all looked so dull and dreary that I rubbed out their clothes and drew Nan and Grandad and Auntie Win and Selina and the other girls in my class and all the teachers in their underwear instead. Then I got scared Nan or Auntie Win might start snooping so I rubbed out all the limp white interlock (my family) and the Marks and Sparks assorted (school staff and pupils) and the scarlet nylon wisps (Selina). I tried to write in proper diary entries but the pages were worn so badly by all this rubbing out that my words blurred into woolly caterpillars.

'I keep a secret journal,' says Selina.

She *doesn't.*

'It's in an elaborate code,' Selina says, smiling, waiting, and then, 'so my parents can't find out all my secrets.'

19

She gets her laugh. He plays along with her.

'What secrets, Selina?'

He knows her name already. She's lying about this secret journal. We made up a code together in the back of the Maths class one day when we were feeling bored, but it was to write secret messages to each other. Selina did once start to write a startling account of her sex life but she got bored bothering with the code and only covered half a page. I know she's never written any kind of diary. But now Robin Campbell is talking to her as if she's a new Virginia Woolf.

The others are starting now too. Celia is actually waving her diary in the air, she's reading out bits about her boyfriend and everyone's laughing except me. I never know how to join in. I'm so different from all the others. They often laugh at me. It's a different sort of laughing from the Celia laughter. That is still bubbling away, the room rocks with the noise, and Robin Campbell glances at the door, as if Miss Beecham might come back and complain.

'Anne Frank writes about her boyfriend a lot too. Listen to this bit,' he says, and starts reading.

He's clever. He's altered the whole mood. He talks about Anne and everyone sobers up and sighs sympathetically.

I've read Anne Frank's diary. It's one of my favourite books. I've taken it out of the library five or six times. I've thought about Anne so much I feel I know her. She's far more of a friend to me than Selina. I sometimes feel like Anne when I'm cooped up with Nan and Grandad and Auntie Win. They often act as if there are Nazis patrolling past our house. They never dream of going out after dark. Nan can get in a state venturing out in broad daylight. She is convinced there is a mugger behind every privet hedge, a rapist lurking in every laburnum. They get so worried if I'm just a little bit late home from school. It isn't just Nan, it's Auntie Win too. And Grandad.

I made Grandad ill the night I went out with Selina

and Bruno and Bruno's friend Mick. I had never been out with any boys before. Bruno and Mick weren't even boys. They were grown up, about to go to college. They looked like students already in their stylishly eccentric clothes. I particularly admired Bruno's jumble sale pinstripe suit and brocade waistcoat. He had naturally fair hair but Selina had bleached it even blonder, and it looked incredible. Mick seemed rather crumpled and mousey by comparison. Mick was supposed to be for me but he seemed much keener on Selina.

We had a meal but I was so shy I didn't say a single word, I was in such a state I could barely swallow. I don't think Mick minded. He talked to Selina most of the time. Bruno tried to be kind to me. He asked me about school and what I planned to do when I left. He looked interested when Selina said I was going to be an artist but then she started talking about her own future and Bruno forgot about me.

I just sat there, pushing food around on my plate, wishing I'd never let Selina persuade me to come. It wasn't a foursome at all. It was a threesome and one person stuck on her own.

I didn't have a watch and I had no idea of the time. Selina knew I'd promised to be back by ten. I whispered that I was worried it was getting late when we went on to the pub but she told me to stop fussing. I drank my bitter lemon and went on worrying, and then the barman came over and asked us to leave because I was obviously under age. The other three argued and I said I had to go home anyway because I was sure it was nearly ten, and Bruno took out a watch from his waistcoat pocket and said it was twenty to eleven.

When I got home at long last Auntie Win opened the door to me.

'Thank God,' she said, and then she leant back against the wall, her legs buckling as if she might faint.

'Are you all right, Auntie Win?'

'*I'm* all right — but take a look at poor old Grandad. Go on, go in the living room. Just see what you've done.

21

I hope you're proud of yourself, young lady.'

Grandad was sitting on the sofa, his head sagging, his legs sprawled. His face was pale grey and glistening with pain.

'Oh Grandad, are you having an attack? I'm sorry, I didn't know the time. Please don't worry any more, I'm home, I'm all right.'

He tried to speak but Nan shushed him fiercely. Her hand was stroking inside his yellow cable cardigan as if she could somehow soothe his heart steady.

'He went out looking for you at half past ten because we were so worried. He got to the top of the road and then his angina started up and he'd left his nitroglycerin tablets at home. He was practically crawling by the time he got back,' said Nan, and she started crying.

I knew she'd never forgive me. Nor would Auntie Win.

Grandad still looked pale at breakfast the next morning but he smiled at me over his porridge.

'It's all right, my old pal, my old beauty.'

Grandad is a great fan of The Archers. He always listens to the omnibus edition when he's having his Sunday bath. He chats back to Phil and Jill and the Grundys and old Walter Gabriel while he soaps and soaks.

'I'm ever so sorry, my old pal, my old beauty,' I mumbled. He likes me to join in the W. Gabriel imitations.

'It's all over now, duckie. Just try not to worry your Nan and Auntie like that again, eh? Here, what does the syrup say?'

He started spooning golden syrup into his bowl, making it spell three shaky syrupy words. I love May. He's been writing it every morning for the last ten years. And then he gives me the syrup spoon so that I can lick it.

Grandad was as sweet as his syrup but Nan was sour all day long, and Auntie Win came up to my bedroom in the evening to have one of her little talks with me.

22

I sat at my mother's blue desk, picking at the brittle paint.

'Don't *do* that, May!' Auntie Win took a deep breath and then gave me an unnerving smile that showed too much of her teeth. 'Now then, pet. I know you think the world of your Grandad and you don't want to make him ill, now do you?'

'I said I'm sorry.'

'I know, dear. But it's so easy to say sorry after the damage has been done.'

'Well, what else can I do? Give Grandad a heart transplant? It's not my fault he's got a bad heart.'

It sounded much ruder than I'd intended. Auntie Win stopped smiling. She sighed. And then she reached for the silver frame on the desk. She showed me the photograph of the girl with long golden hair and big blue eyes and her sweet sweet smile.

'I don't think Mummy would be very happy if she could hear that tone of voice, dear.'

I shut my eyes. I didn't want to look at my mother. I knew her blue eyes were looking straight at me. I wished there was some way I could stop her watching me.

She always watches. After all it's her room, her desk, her bed, her books. When I sit down at her dressing table I always expect to see her face reflected in the mirror, smiling straight through me. Some days I can shut her up in her room. Other days she seeps out and watches wherever I go.

She watches me in the classroom. I'm sure she's watching now, sighing because I never dare say a word and yet she was always such an articulate and intelligent pupil, a delight to teach. I know her school reports off by heart.

I draw a heart on the cover of my school jotter. And then I draw a jumper round it, and hands and legs and a head. I draw in glasses and a smiley mouth. Smile at me. SMILE AT ME. I fill in the heart with black ink until my pen pierces the cover. I look up. Robin Campbell has stopped talking. He's looking at me. He's smiling.

'What's your name?'

'May.'

'Have you ever kept a diary, May?'

'I–I used to. But not any more.'

'Why?'

I shrug the way the other girls do. I expect him to lose interest. But he's still looking, still smiling.

'How about starting one up again? Just for this week. Will you, May?' He doesn't wait for me to answer. 'How about all of you keeping a diary this week? Then we could discuss your entries next time I see you. How about it?'

There are grumbles. Mr Campbell, you're not supposed to set us homework, are you. We'll be getting proper English essays to write as well. Do we have to do this diary, Mr Campbell? Do we have to do a whole *week*?

He laughs. 'Okay. A day. A day in your life. Like the back page of the Sunday Times colour supplement. You know.'

I don't know. But it doesn't really matter. I look down at my book and dab the black ink heart. It worked like a charm.

# Chapter 3

## A DAY IN THE LIFE OF MAY MADDOX

Grandad wakes me up at quarter to seven with a cup of tea. I'd much sooner sleep on, I don't even like tea very much, but early morning cups are a ritual in our house. Grandad has been getting up and making the early morning cup of tea ever since he was married. He's not very well now and he gets out of breath trudging up and down the stairs with the tea tray but he would get very upset if his position as Tea-maker (Early morning) was usurped. So I sit up in bed and read a book and sip my unwanted tea. It's always much too sweet. I used to like lots of sugar when I was a little girl. I don't like any sugar at all now but Grandad can't seem to believe this. Sometimes when he's feeling particularly fond of me he shakes in three or four heaped spoonfuls.

I wait until I hear Nan come out of the bathroom and then I get up and get washed. Grandad waits to wash until after breakfast. My Auntie Win washes after me. She usually taps on the door while I'm in the bathroom and asks me if I'm in there. She knows I'm in there. She means Hurry Up.

25

Nan makes a proper cooked breakfast, bacon, egg and fried tomatoes, and toast with Rose's lime marmalade, and if it's cold she always prepares porridge. She makes me eat it all up. She gives me sandwiches to eat in break too. She takes it as a personal insult that I'm so small and skinny.

I go to school at eight o'clock. I used to travel on the bus with Auntie Win but she retired from work last year and so now she just stays at home with Nan and Grandad. I generally get to school about twenty to nine. I talk to my best friend Selina.

Then school starts. I like Art. I am going to be an artist when I grow up. I quite like English and the Library lesson is all right. I don't like any of the other lessons though. I hate P.E. most of all. We have Gymn on Mondays, Netball on Wednesdays and Double Hockey on Friday mornings. I always pray for rain on Fridays.

Today, Monday 7th January, the first day back at school, we miss French first lesson because we're having a long assembly and a hymn book check and instead of our English lesson we have a writer come to talk to us. Robin Campbell. He talks to us about writing diaries and he reads to us and asks us to write our own diary. This. And he's obviously going to want to read what we think of him. And I'm not going to put what I really think. I don't want him to know. And I don't want him to know about Nan and Grandad and Auntie Win either. Or me. So I'm going to tear up this rubbish and try again.

Only I don't like my days. I don't like my
life. I don't like being me.
 So.


## A DAY IN THE LIFE OF SELINA MURRAY?


I'd much sooner be Selina. It still seems so odd that she's
my best friend. I got so used to her being my worst enemy.
When we were first years and had to sit next to each other in
Register order she took an instant dislike to me. She
nudged me with her sharp elbows, she barged in front of
me, she stole my sandwiches, she scribbled all over my
exercise books, she imitated the way I talked. She didn't
take so much notice of me when we no longer had to sit
together but she was sometimes still so hateful she reduced
me to tears.

 So my heart sank when I bumped into her at the
National Gallery last Summer. I was there with Auntie
Win. She takes me to an Art gallery every holiday. She
doesn't care for galleries herself, and her feet start playing
her up, but she considers it vital for my artistic education.
She would never let me go to London on my own, of course.
So there we were, plodding round the paintings together,
Auntie Win's footsteps embarrassingly emphatic because
her arches were aching and she'd changed into her Dr
Scholl exercise sandals. We had worked our way through
the art of four whole centuries when I heard someone calling my name.

 'May! Well well. Fancy seeing you here.'

 Selina looked terribly grown up and glamorous in a
white sweater, white jeans and gold high heeled sandals.

Her skin was gold too, a smooth golden tan all over. I was wearing a crumpled cotton frock and was as white as ever, apart from my nose, which was scarlet and shredding after I'd dared to sit for half an hour in the garden.

I said hello to Selina and then tried to hurry past her before she worked out I was with my old Auntie. But Auntie Win saw us talking and came clacking over.

'Who's your friend, May? Aren't you going to introduce me?'

I muttered introductions, blushing. Auntie Win looked very surprised when I said Selina was in my class at school.

'Are you on your own, dear? Isn't that a bit lonely? Would you like to come round the gallery with us?' She said it as if she actually thought she was doing Selina a favour.

I was amazed when Selina agreed. I found out later she'd just had a row with Bruno and stormed off, and now she wanted to attach herself to us to show him she didn't care. He must have been watching as she circled several galleries, making clever remarks about colour and composition that impressed Auntie Win no end. They impressed me too. I was the one who was going to be the artist and yet Selina seemed to know much more about it than I did.

Auntie Win's arches gave out altogether in the French 18th century, so she sat on a seat and rested her feet on top of her sandals. They looked very flat and floppy, like boiled plaice. Selina sauntered round the room on her little gold heels while I stumped along at her side. Auntie Win kept winking at me to show how pleased she was that I seemed to have a friend at long last. I prayed Selina would think Auntie Win's winks a nervous tic.

Selina started showing off in front of a big Fragonard painting, pronouncing the name in a very grand French way.

'I suppose you've read lots of Art History books,' I said shyly.

'Do me a favour,' said Selina. 'No, it's Bruno, my boyfriend. He did it for one of his A-levels. He's been a right

28

bore, always dragging me round all these paintings. He did "Images of Sexuality in French 18th Century Painting" for his special project.'

I stared at the painting of the pink and white woman simpering on cushions, her dimpled knees disconcertingly spread. I felt very undermined. I wasn't even acquainted with twentieth century English images of sexuality. This Fragonard woman's sexuality seemed menacing. Even her delicate ear became an alarming red orifice.

'It's very rude.'

'Oh May, you are a baby. There are some really rude Fragonards somewhere, too shocking to be on display. But this is nothing. Just because she's got bare tits.'

'It's not that. Look at her ear.'

'Her *ear*?' Selina burst out laughing. But then she looked. And she saw what I meant.

'You are weird, May,' she said, still giggling, but she nodded as if I'd unexpectedly passed a test.

She wanted me to go and have a coffee with her in some cakeshop in Soho but Auntie Win looked so appalled that even Selina could see there was no point persisting. She went off by herself saying she'd give me a ring. She phoned me the very next day. We met up most days after that and when we went back to school we had somehow become best friends.

Auntie Win and Nan were disconcerted. They had always worried because I didn't have proper friends. Selina was from 'a good home' and she 'spoke nicely' so she seemed suitable. Auntie Win had been impressed, but she did say Selina was very sophisticated — and when she called round at my house in one of her tight little skirts and tarty stilettos Nan went white. But Grandad took to Selina straight away.

'She seems a lovely little lass,' he declared. 'I think she'll be a very good friend for our May. She'll bring her out of herself.'

I'm not any good at coming out of myself. I stay safely inside. I'm not going to start sending out dispatches on my daily life to Robin Campbell.

And yet I've got to hand in something next Monday. I don't want him to think I'm too lazy or too thick to do any work. I've got to think of a way round things. I am supposed to have imagination.

## A DAY IN THE LIFE OF MAY MADDOX

I've tried that.

So how about:

## A NIGHT IN THE LIFE OF MAY MADDOX

Midnight. Monday January 7th starts. I don't hear the clock chiming. I'm asleep under my old-fashioned quilt. My mother slept under the same quilt when she was my age. Her mother made it from scraps of her own dresses. When I look at Nan now in her beige and brown I can't imagine her in pink flowered lawn, harlequin diamonds, shiny green taffeta. When did she wear all these pretty dresses? My Nan going to parties! I dream about those parties. Did my mother dream about them too? Do we ever join hands in our sleep like a pair of paper dolls and go to a party together? Do we tuck the little white tags on our dresses over our shoulders and smooth our paper frills? Do we dance up and down, pointing our paper toes? No, there are scissors in my dream, the Strewelpeter book is open on my shelf, the long-legged scissor man is loping towards us.

Snip snap. We are severed, our paper limbs
limp with the shock. My mother floats away,
our dresses flying after her like a flock of
birds. I catch just one of the dresses and
smooth it out and try to write on the back of
it. I have to write a diary entry. My paper
dress shrinks into a small notebook. I pick up
a pen and start writing but the notebook is
still shrinking. It's as small as a matchbox
now. Meanwhile my pen is getting bigger.
Much bigger. I have to hold it with two
hands to control it. I try to squeeze one letter
onto each little page but when I've written
the three letters of my name the notebook is
only a postage stamp and the pen is the size
of a broom handle. It is a broom, a sturdy
broom with bristles, and I climb astride. It
jerks me up into the air and then whizzes
round and round my bedroom. The bristles
sweep all the books and photographs and
mirrors to the floor. The sharp twigs tear at
the curtains. We smash right through the
window and I scream. I wake up and I'm
lying under my old-fashioned patchwork
quilt and it's Monday 7th January and time
to get up for school.

I have to read it out. He's left me till last. The bell's
going to go any minute. I wish it would. I know I'm
blushing. I should have written a normal day like everyone else. I'm going to make a fool of myself and they'll
all laugh. He'll laugh too.

I gabble through it. My cheeks are still burning when
I sit down. Silence. Selina is looking at me, frowning.
The others look puzzled, wondering what it was all
about. They think I'm weird. What does Robin Campbell think? What do I care what he thinks, who cares, I
care —

'I thought that was —'

And the bell goes. The girls stand up, laughing, talking, rushing off to the next lesson. I fold my paper into a tight little square and stand up. I walk as calmly as I can past his desk. I know he's watching me. I don't dare look at him.

'May?' He says it quietly. I'm not certain he's spoken. I glance at him, going red. Oh God, why do I always burn like a beacon?

'Don't you want to know what I think about it?'

'Well–I–the bell's gone and —'

'And there's me kidding myself you'd be desperate to know,' he says. He's joking. Well, I think he's joking.

'I do. I would. But —'

'Your life is ruled by the bell.'

'No. Only I'll get into trouble. It's games next, and —'

'Games. Do you like games?'

'No.'

'I once went a whole term with my ankle in thick bandages, pretending I'd strained it, just so I could get out of football.'

I giggle. Do I dare tell him?

'I used to make out I had a migraine. Then I got to lie in the sick room. Sometimes I even smuggled a book in with me.'

'You enterprising girl. Well. Have you got a migraine coming on right this minute?'

'I daren't. She started to get very suspicious.'

'Oh. Well I'd better let you go. Hell hath no fury like a Games Teacher in a tantrum.'

'Yes. Only ... I would like to know. What you think.'

'Well, tell you what. Shall we have a chat about it at lunchtime? How long do you take to nosh your stew and spotted dick?'

'It's all hamburger and chips now.'

'Oh no! I was so looking forward to school dinners. Don't you even get jam roly poly any more?'

'Yoghurt and apples.'

32

He pulls a face. Then he smiles. 'Quarter past one? Here?'

'Quarter past one. Here,' I repeat.

# Chapter 4

'Read it again for me.'

I smooth out the paper, clear my throat, and whisper the first few sentences. It's much more difficult alone with him. I stammer over the word 'mother'. I hum demented ems, blushing.

'I'll read it,' he says gently, taking it from me. He reads it himself, but it sounds odd, his voice saying my words. He stops and smiles at me sympathetically. 'I feel stupid,' he says, and when he carries on he reads in a quick mumble. He nods every so often and then sighs when he gets to the end. 'You know it's good, don't you?'

I shrug, delighted.

'Do you want to write when you grow up?'

'Me, write? No, I'm going to be an artist.'

'Oh.' He looks surprised. Disappointed. He peers at the paintings pinned on the wall.

'Where's yours?'

'It's the street scene. And that's my drawing too, the one of the seashells.'

I worked on them all last term. If I close my eyes I can still see the yellow-green of the trees, the zig-zag pattern of the rooftops, the check of the bricks, oh the agony of filling in all those fiddly little bricks. And the seashells took weeks too, shading every single crevice and curlicue.

He walks over and examines them.

'They're not very good.'

I don't know what to say.

'They're dull.'

'I–I came top in the Art exam.'

'I bet you came top in English too.'

'No. I came fifth.'

'Oh well. Schools are dotty places. So. They've conned you into thinking you're an artist?'

'I've always wanted to be an artist. My mother was. And so I've always wanted to be an artist too.'

He comes back and sits beside me, looking interested.

'I wouldn't have thought you'd have wanted to copy your mother,' he says. 'I thought you wanted to snip right through the umbilical cord.'

I don't even see what he means for a second. Then I start.

'That was just in the dream.'

'It wasn't a real dream though. That was too literary for any old dream. You made it up, didn't you?'

'Yes, all right, but —'

He's looking at my writing again.

'It's fantastic. I love the witchy bits.'

'There aren't any witchy bits,' I say anxiously.

'Yes, there are. Broomsticks, flying, magic, what more do you want? Don't you like witches? I'm thinking about reading *The Crucible* with your class. It's a play about the Salem witch hunts. You haven't seen it, have you? It's been on television. I think your sixth form did it for their GCSE's so Miss Beecham's got lots of spare copies. She wants me to do "a book-related project" with your form, and she doesn't feel like forking out school funds on thirty copies of Robin Campbell when thirty Robert Campbells are already gathering dust in the school cupboard. She wanted me to use them but I can't stick old Robert Campbell's books.'

'I didn't like *The Time of the Terror*. There was so much torture.' I swallow. 'They tortured witches, didn't they?'

'Yes, they did. But don't worry. *The Crucible* doesn't

35

go in for gloating descriptions of toe-nail tweaking. I thought we could start reading it next week. And then maybe we could do some witch projects? We could do a straight history of witchcraft. We could make up some spells, write some Occult stories. What do you think, May?'

'Mmm.' I wonder what he'd say if I told him I'm a witch. And I can work my own spells.

'You sound a bit lukewarm. Come on, you don't have to be on your best behaviour with me.'

'I think it's an interesting idea,' I say cautiously.

'You are a polite girl.' I think he's laughing at me. 'You see, I really want to get things going, get people reading, writing, using a bit of imagination. I thought the diary thing was a bit of a flop. It was my fault, I tried to pack too much in last week, reading bits here, bits there, and there isn't enough time, I mean, forty minutes, I ask you. You just get started and it's time to stop, and everyone leaps up and out the moment that bell goes. And I mucked up the timing today too. We spent ages discussing those dinky little diary entries. I slept in so Dad drove me to school and I came top in History or bottom in Biology and I went shopping at lunchtime and I bought a new record — on and on, every girl a clone of the one before and then at last you read out your smashing surreal piece and that bloody bell goes.'

'You didn't read from your own book.'

'True. I always say I can't stick writers reading their own work, and yet I'd brought it with me, as you noticed, maybe hoping for the "Oh sir, please sir, read us your boy's diary, sir".'

He's very good at imitating girls' voices.

'Can I read it?'

He laughs.

'No, I really want to.'

He hands it over. There are two boys on the cover. One is in old-fashioned school uniform, a cap and a striped blazer and a scarf; the other's wearing jeans and a Snoopy teeshirt. They're standing back to back but they're looking round at each other. I open the book and slide my eyes down the first page. It's about this boy who's listening to his mother and stepfather. He doesn't seem to like either of them very much. They're talking about him. It doesn't sound as if they think much of him either. They're in their bedroom. He's in his. Then they start making love and he covers his ears, burning. I burn too, reading. He couldn't have read this out in class.

'You can take it home if you like.'

I'm going to have to hide it somehow. Nan would have a fit.

'Thank you.'

The bell goes. I twitch but then hold myself still. He laughs again.

'You poor girl. Go on. I'm not mean enough to make you late again.'

'It's only the first bell. It's not lessons for another five minutes.'

'God, what a system. You didn't get into trouble with your P.E. teacher, did you?'

'Oh no. Well. A bit.'

'Didn't you blame me?'

'I tried to, but Miss French doesn't listen to excuses.'

'Oh dear. Did you get sentenced to a bout of running on the spot? That used to be my games master's favourite punishment. You'd run until you felt you were going to go straight through those shiny floorboards, like Rumpelstiltskin.'

'I always felt so sorry for Rumpelstiltskin. He helped that stupid girl spin all her gold and yet she wasn't a bit grateful.'

'Absolutely. It's always the odd and the ugly who suffer in fairy tales. Fine if you're a fairy, tough if you're a freak.'

'And the princesses always have long golden hair.'

'Witches have red hair,' he says, smiling.

'I'd sooner be a princess.'

'Princesses are pretty. Witches are powerful. Wouldn't you sooner be powerful than pretty?'

'Some people get to be both,' I say, thinking of Selina. 'It's not fair.'

'True. Life isn't fair. Like Fairy Tales.'

The second bell rings.

'Off you go. I'll see you next week. And don't worry if you don't get on with my book. My own daughter says it's boring.'

A daughter. I'd somehow not even imagined him married. And a daughter makes him much older.

'I'd sooner you wrote something more for me. Will you?'

'What sort of thing?'

'Anything you like. If you don't go a bundle on witches then what about fairies? Write me your own fairy tale.'

'All right. I'll try. Although I want to read your book too.'

'You are a writer, you know. Don't waste your time with art. After all, you've got one artist in your family already.'

'No we haven't.'

'Your mother.'

'Well. She's dead.'

I walk out of the classroom and all through afternoon school I think about my fairy story. I start writing as soon as I get home.

There was once a beautiful Princess who lived in a golden castle with her doting parents and an old aunt who acted as a governess. The Princess was as golden as her castle. She let down her long hair over the battlements and admirers threaded daisies and buttercups through the shining locks. They begged the Princess to come out of the golden castle but she never would. She

smiled at them sweetly but she shook her
hair free of their flowers. At dusk she swept
up her hair, coiled it neatly in a golden
crown on top of her head, and went inside
the castle. She assured her doting family that
she would never be charmed away from the
golden castle but every night in her turret
room she would paint a portrait of a
handsome Prince. She was so talented a
painter that the governess felt inadequate
instructing her so the Royal Family hired a
special tutor, an impoverished young artist.
The Princess started when she saw him. He
looked exactly like her portrait of the
imaginary Prince. She couldn't *help* falling in
love with him. He threaded rosebuds and
forget-me-nots throughout her long hair,
and hung ripe cherries on her tiny ears. The
Royal Family were distraught when they saw
their Princess, fragrant with crushed flowers,
stained with sweet juice. But the Princess
seemed so very happy they tried to rejoice for
her sake. They prepared an elaborate
wedding feast and the Princess and the artist
made their vows and went to live in a city
garret many miles away from the golden
palace. It seemed very empty without the
Princess. The very gold tarnished.

Then the Princess sent word that she was
going to have a child. But the Princess did
not bloom. The spring went from her step.
Her long locks lost their shine and seemed
thinner every day. Strands spiralled to the
ground as she walked, enough to bind into a
long golden cord. The artist was very
frightened. He picked the Princess up in his
arms and carried her all the way to the
golden palace. He begged the Royal Family
to help him take care of her. They put their

darling child to bed and nursed her tenderly but the Princess grew steadily weaker. The child within her seemed to sap all her strength.

Then the Princess started screaming in great pain. She screamed hour after hour until at last the child was born. It was not a tiny golden Princess. It was a mewling goblin creature with hair the colour of hellfire. As it burst into the world the Princess gave one last gasp and died. The artist flung himself on her breast and wept. The King and the Queen clung to each other in their despair. The governess cried brokenly. The newborn child cried too but no-one could bear to touch it.

They buried the Princess in the palace garden, planting a willow by the graveside. The artist lay on top of the grave, whispering through the earth to his decaying love. He could not endure their separation. He took the long golden cord of hair and hung himself from the willow tree. The King and the Queen and the governess grew stooped and silent with grief. Dust carpeted the marble floors of the golden palace. Spider's webs grew thick as nets. The only sound was the constant wailing of the goblin child. Oh how it wailed.

'What are you writing, dear?'
I fold the paper in half.
'It's private.'
Auntie Win shakes her head at me.
'I'm not trying to pry, pet. I'm simply interested. You've been pulling such funny faces as you've been writing. I wonder if you might need glasses, you know.'
'I had my eyes tested at school. They're fine.'

'Anyway, if that's not homework I think it might be a good idea to put it away for now and do some painting instead. That portrait won't be finished until we're all in our dotage.'

'Speak for yourself, Win. I feel in my dotage already,' says Nan, putting down her knitting with a groan and flexing her fingers.

'What are you on about, Annie? You're still a slip of a girl,' says Grandad. 'A little slip. My Annie petticoat.'

'May! Go and get your paints,' Auntie Win says sharply.

'I don't feel like painting, not this evening.'

'You've only had those lovely oil paints five minutes. Don't say you're sick of them already,' Auntie Win hisses, her face close to mine so that I smell her breath. 'You'll hurt Grandad's feelings,' she mouths.

Nan and Grandad gave me the oil paints for Christmas. And brushes and turpentine and linseed oil and ten specially prepared canvasses. Grandad even made me an easel, a board tacked to the back of an old chair. Nan sewed one of Grandad's old shirts into a special painting smock and cut up an even older shirt into squares for painting rags. It is the most elaborate present they have ever given me. They usually give me a diary and something like a fountain pen or a wristwatch. And the new volume of my mother's diary. Only there isn't one this year. She stopped writing them when she was my age. She spent all her spare time painting. She had oil paints for *her* fifteenth Christmas present. She took all her painting things away with her when she got married. Otherwise I daresay I'd have been given her dried-up tubes of paint, her stubby brushes, her screwed-up painting rags.

Her first proper oil painting was a portrait. It hangs in the living room above the fireplace. It's like a mirror reflecting the past. Grandad and Nan sit on the carefully painted sofa, the same dull cracking leather sofa, but she's done a highlight or two to show off the gleam of the leather when it was new. Grandad ponders the *Telegraph* crossword, his lips pursed as if he's testing each

41

word for flavour. He looks bare without his glasses. And where is the big soft stomach that makes him look like Dr Doolittle? This Grandad looks like a real man. And Nan looks positively girlish at the other end of the sofa. She's knitting, of course, but her head is at a perky angle and there's a bright lipstick smile on her face. She's wearing silly fluffy slippers with high heels to show off her trim ankles. The days of surgical bandages and bunions are far in the future. Auntie Win sits in the armchair at the edge of the portrait. She's wearing her office clothes, a dark suit and little white blouse, and her hair is pinned up in a pleat. She looks as if the pins are digging right into her.

They thought it would be a lovely idea for me to paint a portrait of them now in exactly the same positions. I spread newspapers on the floor to protect the carpet, set up my makeshift easel and pull the painting smock over my head. Grandad and Nan and Auntie Win sit stiffly, as if they can actually feel the little dabs of my paintbrush. I have blocked in the background and the basic shapes of the three figures. I am ready to start putting in the details.

I don't want to. The smell of the oil paints makes me feel sick. My eyes water as I stare and stare at the three figures. I dab and waver and wipe. It's no use. I try so hard but I can't seem to manage it any more.

Robin Campbell is right. I'm not really that good at painting. I don't even want to paint. Why have I got to be an artist?

I sigh out loud. I mix white and black and start to paint Grandad's grey eyebrows. I strain to get them right, using the very tip of my brush, but Grandad's stupid easel jerks as I dab and a great grey worm writhes right across his face.

I sigh again.

'This easel,' I mutter.

Grandad seems deep in his crossword clues. But Auntie Win is frowning, Nan is looking worried. I mustn't upset Grandad, oh dear me no. I must stay meek little May and go on painting and pretending. Only I'm so sick sick sick of being good.

I want to be bad.

I coat my brush with black paint. It goes dab dab at the canvas. Grandad hasn't got any eyebrows now. He hasn't even got a face. There's just a black gap where his head used to be.

It unnerves me. I take one of my little painting rags and wipe all the black away before they can see what I've done. I wipe and wipe but black is a difficult colour. Grandad gets his head back but he looks very grey in the face, as if he's having one of his attacks.

# Chapter 5

'It's him.'

'Who?'

'Who do you *think*?'

He sees us and smiles, standing at the door of the Waggon and Horses.

'Hello. Where are you two off to then?'

Selina tosses her gleaming hair and giggles. 'Oh, we're just going to have a look round the shops.' She pauses, giggles again. 'But we don't mind having a drink first, do we, May?'

Robin laughs at her. It's very cold so he's wearing an old cream Arran sweater that comes right up to his chin. It would look silly on anyone else but it looks fine on him. He can even get away with that long red scarf. He should have gloves to match. His hands are white and bloodless. They're smallish for a man. Sensitive. He rubs them together briskly.

'My God, it's freezing. I'd love to buy you both a whisky to warm you up but I'm not sure what your headmistress would say.'

Selina giggles yet again. I try too. My face is split in a stupid grin. I want to say something witty and wry but the words won't come. There is beginning to be a silence. Selina is manipulating it, staring up at him, her smile challenging. She knows exactly how to part her lips and preen. I want him to raise an eyebrow, to back away, to look at me and laugh. But he looks as if he's all set to join the Selina Murray fan club.

'Come on, Selina,' I mumble, breaking the spell.

She looks annoyed and then shrugs one shoulder and smiles at him as if they've got some kind of secret.

'See you around,' she says, as if Robin Campbell is one of her boyfriends.

We walk off. I wonder if he's watching us, Selina all bobbing hair and sexy bottom as she struts on her non-regulation high heels, me six inches shorter, with my pigtail and my duffle coat down to my calves.

'He's quite sweet,' says Selina, as we turn the corner.

'Mmm.'

'A bit dated. That scarf! But he's got sexy eyes. And I do like his glasses, don't you?'

'Mmm.'

Selina hums a pop song until we get to the High Street.

'I want to go to Miss Selfridge. I'm looking for something to wear to this party on Saturday.'

'Mmm.'

Selina is always going to parties, always buying new clothes.

'What's up with you?'

'What?' Selina doesn't usually expect me to make much response. We both accept the fact that stylish new clothes and parties cannot concern me.

'What did he say to you yesterday?'

'Who?'

'Who! Don't start that again.'

I knew it had annoyed Selina, Robin asking me to see him yesterday lunchtime. She had deliberately not asked me about it during afternoon school. I hadn't realised it was still annoying her. I can't see why. He didn't ask me about my writing just now. He didn't even ask how I'm getting on with his book.

'What did you talk about?'

'Nothing much. He just went over my diary thing.'

'Yes, why did you write all that weird dream stuff?'

'I don't know. I just felt like it.'

'Did you get it out of a book or something?'

'No.'

'It didn't sound your sort of thing. I suppose it impressed him?'

I shrug. It *did* — but it didn't make him look at me the way he looked at Selina just now.

'What else did he say?'

'We talked a bit about fairy stories.'

'Typical!' says Selina. 'Here, I want to go into Smiths.'

She buys herself a Mars bar, a Double Decker, and a packet of salt and vinegar crisps. Selina's lunch. And she never gets spots, never needs fillings. I have brown bread salad sandwiches, limp and depressing. Selina gobbles up her Mars bar as she stands at the magazine rack, having a free flick through *Vogue* and *Just Seventeen*. My mouth waters. I would give anything for a Mars but I can't afford it. Grandad gives me 50 pence a week pocket money. It's not that he's mean, he just doesn't realise how much things cost nowadays.

Two sixth form boys from Fitzwilliam are looking at Selina as if *she* is a Mars bar. They whisper and nudge each other idiotically. Selina's pink tongue searches for a crumb of chocolate. They chortle. She gives a little smile and changes magazines. *Smash Hits*, a clever choice. It gives the boys the courage to approach her.

'Here, do you like that group?' One of the boys points at a photograph.

Selina shrugs. 'They're okay.'

'I think they're great. Although I thought their last record was a right rip off.'

They discuss it. The other boy tries to join in. Selina-Mars-bar melts, oozing sticky charm. They eye her greedily. They've forgotten me.

'What did you think of that record, May?' Selina asks, smiling so sweetly.

The boys stare at me apprehensively. Two and two equals four. One of them will get off with Selina. And therefore the other one will get lumbered with me. But they look at Selina with resigned respect. They think

she's so sweet bringing me into the act. Selina isn't
sweet. She knows I've never heard this record, never
even heard of this group. Our radio at home is only ever
tuned in to Radio Four. We don't even know it as
Radio Four in my family; Nan and Grandad and
Auntie Win still call it the Home Service.

'It's all right, I suppose,' I mutter.

I don't know why I'm even trying. I don't like either
of these boys. I don't like Selina either. I know she's trying to make me look a fool. She succeeds.

They start talking about some pop star with a girl's
name and I'm not cautious enough. I say 'she'. They
stare and start spluttering and I realise it's a boy.
There's no point trying now.

They arrange to meet Selina this evening outside
Macdonalds.

'Catch me hanging round a hamburger bar all evening!' she says, as soon as we walk out of Smiths. 'How
old do they think I am, *twelve*? They weren't that
wonderful, were they? May? Oh God, are you sulking?
Come on, don't be like that.'

'Why do you have to flirt with those stupid boys if
you don't even like them?'

'Because it's fun,' says Selina, linking arms. 'Come
and help me choose this dress, eh?'

'Hadn't we better get back?'

'We've got ages yet and even if we're late, it's only
English. I bet Miss Beecham won't even notice if we're
not there.'

'You know she will.'

'Just two minutes in Miss Selfridge, that's all.'

'Well, you go. I'll go back,' I say, unlinking my arm.

'You are a pain, May,' says Selina, but she comes
with me. She licks her Double Decker like an ice lolly.
'Come after school with me, then.'

'You know they worry if I'm late.'

'You are daft with your Grandma and that old
Auntie. You're going to have to learn to stand up to
them some time.'

'You know I'm not very good at standing up to people.'

She laughs and offers me the other half of her Double Decker.

'Here. Have a little nosh. Maybe I'll leave Miss Selfridge anyway. I'll see if I can screw some more cash out of my Dad, and then I'll go to Whistles. What shall I have, a dress? Or what about trousers and a sexy sort of top?'

'I don't know why you fuss so much about your clothes. From what you've said about these parties of yours you end up taking them all off.'

'You know you ought to go really mad and come to a party or two yourself. It would do you the world of good. You can't stay a little girl for the rest of your life. Honestly, you're so *weird*. I don't want to be nasty but look at your *hair*. And those awful flat shoes. Now come on, you don't *have* to wear stuff like that. Haven't you got any heels at all? Shall I look you out a pair of mine? There are those patent things, I never wear them now, and —'

'Selina. I wouldn't be allowed to. Parties, shoes, all of it. You know I wouldn't.'

'I bet you've never asked. Look, how about if I ask for you?'

'No!'

She nags me all the way back to school. The last bell has gone. We are five minutes late for English and Miss Beecham gives us both a telling off. Selina doesn't seem to care. I wish I didn't. I want Miss Beecham to like me. I want to be good at English. Although the highest I've ever come is fifth. Once I got no marks at all for an essay because Miss Beecham said I hadn't kept to the title.

Miss Beecham would have given me 0 out of 20 for my diary piece. And doubtless 0 out of 20 for my stupid changeling story. Maybe Robin Campbell won't like it either. I'm not sure whether I've got the nerve to show it to him now. He'll think it's stupid. Although why should a story always make sense? And he said I can write. He says I am a writer.

I'm not much good at the Miss Beecham school of writing. 'A Train Journey.' 'Winter Landscape.' 'The Advantages of Learning Foreign Languages.' I was much better in the junior school when we simply made up stories. I can do that. I used to get into trouble for it. I'd tell Nan about my imaginary friends and all our adventures and she'd frown and tell me to stop being silly. It was always nonsense to Nan but not Auntie Win. I think it all started when she discovered me downstairs with my hand in the biscuit tin in the middle of the night. I blurted out a story to stop her being cross with me. I said someone had taken my hand and pulled me out of bed and danced me downstairs to the kitchen. Someone young and pretty, with long flowing hair. Someone who said she was so hungry she could eat up all the biscuits in the tin, especially the flapjacks. I knew Auntie Win's flapjacks had always been my mother's favourites. That's why she went on baking them for me, although I like shop biscuits better.

'Who was this someone? What colour hair did she have? What else did she say?'

Auntie Win was a sucker for my stories. I made up as many as I could, and I manufactured a few dreams. It wasn't long before she started talking about the Other Side and children acting as unconscious mediums. Even Nan started questioning me about my so-called dreams. It was Grandad who took me aside one day and said 'Enough's enough, my old pal, my old beauty. Stop going on about these dreams of yours. It's getting your Nannie and your Auntie in a right old tiz-woz. I don't know whether it's real or whether it's pretend. All I know is that it's best left unsaid.'

So I haven't said it since — but now when I write for Robin it bubbles out almost by itself.

Selina keeps passing me notes in English about this party. And in Geography and General Music. And when we come out of school she links arms with me

49

again, walking along beside me, although she lives in the opposite direction.

'What are you playing at, Selina?'

'I told you. I'm going to ask your Ninny Nanny if you can come to this party.'

'You *can't*.'

She can. She comes all the way home with me. She waits while I knock at the door. Oh God, it isn't a game. She's really going to ask. I don't know what on earth I'm going to do. She'll talk a whole load of lies and fool Nan and she'll say I can go and I'll be stuck at Selina's party, the Comic Turn of all time. Selina knocks now. I don't know why Nan's not coming. I knock again and at last the door opens.

'Nan?'

It's not Nan, it's Auntie Win. She's shaking. She can't even speak. But she mouths one word.

'Grandad!'

# Chapter 6

'I'll be off,' Selina says hurriedly.

I try to catch hold of her arm but she's gone. I want to run too. Auntie Win pulls me inside and shuts the door. It's very dark in the hall and I can barely see her. She's gasping as if she's running round the room but she's standing absolutely still.

'Yes, it's Grandad,' she whispers. She makes a little choking sound. 'He's gone.'

She means he's dead. Dead dead dead. I shriek it inside my head. I can't bear it. I can't let it be true.

'What do you mean, *gone*?' I demand. 'Where's he gone? What do you mean?'

'Oh May,' say Auntie Win, and she starts crying. 'Poor Grandad's —'

'Don't say it!' I shout.

Auntie Win wraps her arms round me. We are not used to embracing and we stand stiffly to attention. Auntie Win pats my shoulder, little helpless taps. I'm suddenly aware of voices in the living room, strange voices.

'Who's that?'

'We've got the police here,' she whispers.

'What?'

I break away and run into the living room. Nan is slumped in a corner of the sofa, her face dissolving. A young policewoman is sitting by her side, and there's a very pink policeman standing awkwardly in front of the standard lamp.

51

'What's happened to Grandad? He–he hasn't been murdered, has he?'

'May!' Auntie Win hisses behind me.

Nan doesn't say anything. She stares at me for a moment as if she doesn't even know who I am. Then she blinks and rubs her brimming eyes.

'I forgot all about you, May. Should we have sent for you? It's too late now. He's gone. Oh dear, he's gone, they've taken him away.'

'Sit down and I'll get you a cup of tea, dear,' says the policewoman, pressing me into a chair.

She's made a pot and set it all out on a tray. She's used the best rose cups with the gold handles but she's set them on the chipped green breakfast saucers. Nan and Auntie Win don't seem to have noticed although they'd normally have a fit.

'Of course Grandad hasn't been murdered,' says the policewoman, giving me a cup of tea. 'Here, dear, take a sip.'

It's stronger than we make it and it's too sugary, the way Grandad ... I put the cup down, spilling some, but no-one bothers to mop at the carpet.

'Your Grandad passed away at lunchtime, love. The doctor says it was a coronary.'

'I put the pill in his mouth, I got it right under his tongue, but it wouldn't *work*,' Auntie Win suddenly sobs. 'So I tried the kiss of life but I don't think I was doing it right, I kept blowing but nothing happened.'

Nan groans and tries to get up. She reaches out her hand. The young policeman goes to help her. Nan looks bewildered. She wasn't reaching for him at all. She was reaching for Grandad.

I burst into tears.

'That's it, pet, have a good cry. It often helps,' says the policewoman. She turns to Auntie Win. 'I take it she lives with you. What about her Mum and Dad?'

'Her mother passed away the day May was born. And her father took his own life six months later.' Auntie Win pauses, trying to stop crying. 'We've never got

52

over it. No wonder poor Arthur started his heart trouble. It was the shock. Amy was the apple of his eye. Well, we all thought the world of her. Like I said, we've never got over it. Well you don't, do you? And now Arthur —'

'Hush now, Win,' says Nan.

Auntie Win can't hush. She starts sobbing hysterically although she's trying to shut her mouth to stop the noise. The policewoman tries holding her but it has no effect.

'I think you'd better take another one of those pills,' she says firmly. 'The doctor left you several, didn't he? Yes, there we are, you swallow it with a sip of tea and then I should go and have a little lie down.'

'I can't lie down, I've got to start getting everything organised and then there's my sister, look at her, she's in a daze — and there's the child —'

'We'll get things sorted out, don't you worry,' says the policewoman, taking hold of Auntie Win's elbow and helping her to her feet.

'I still don't know why you're here. You can't believe there's anything *suspect*?'

'Of course not. We did try to explain,' says the policewoman patiently. 'It's just routine, love. We always have to come when someone dies — well, unless they've just been to the doctors.'

Grandad hasn't just been to the doctor. He hasn't had a bad attack since before Christmas. He was fine until . . . Until.

The policewoman goes upstairs with Auntie Win. We hear her sobbing overhead. It's very quiet in here. The policeman clears his throat, at a loss. Nan sniffs softly. The clock on the mantelpiece ticks away as if it's a perfectly ordinary afternoon. Grandad always ticked too, when I curled up on his lap as a little girl. I loved taking his pocket watch out and playing with it while Grandad pretended to be the White Rabbit in *Alice*. He'd twitch his nose like a rabbit and try to wiggle his ears. He did it to amuse me only the other day and I just sighed and

53

said I wasn't a baby any more.

Oh Grandad, I want you so.

'Where is he?' I ask.

The policeman looks at me worriedly. He glances at Nan but I don't think she's even heard.

'They fetched him away as soon as possible,' says the policeman. 'It's best that way. He'll be at the undertakers.'

I think of Grandad being undressed like a great doll, wrapped in a long white shroud, and put to bed in a coffin. Will they take off his glasses? And what about his false teeth? I've always hated the way his mouth goes without them. I can't ask about his teeth, they'll think I'm mad.

The policewoman comes back without Auntie Win.

'She's having a lie down. I expect she'll nod off for quite a while, those pills are quite strong. But I think it's for the best, don't you?'

She's talking to Nan but Nan is busy with her own thoughts.

'We'd better be going now,' says the policewoman, looking at Nan doubtfully. Then she looks at me.

'You haven't got an Auntie or anyone who could come for a few days, have you, dear?'

'I've just got Auntie Win. Well, she's my Great Aunt really.'

'How about if we go and fetch one of the neighbours in to keep an eye on you and your Grannie?'

'We don't really know them properly. We don't sort of ... mix,' I say helplessly.

'Oh well, you seem a very sensible girl, of course you'll be all right,' says the policewoman. She lowers her voice. 'Don't worry if your Gran seems a bit funny. It's the shock, it often affects folk like this. I should call the doctor in again tomorrow, just to make sure.'

I see them to the door. I don't know what to do when they're gone. I don't want to go in the living room with Nan. I don't want to go upstairs with Auntie Win. I don't want either of them, I want Grandad.

54

I can't hover in the hall for ever. I go into the living room. Nan is still sitting, sniffing, staring into space.

'Oh Nan.' I run to her.

She looks startled. I sit beside her, trying to cuddle into her. She feels so little I'm scared of squashing her.

'What are we going to do?'

She doesn't answer.

'Nan! Do we have to get a certificate or something? And do we have to go to a solicitor?'

She sniffs again.

'We'll leave all that to your Grandad, dear. He always takes care of business matters.'

I straighten up and stare at her.

'*Nan!*'

'What, dear?'

I don't know what to say.

'Nothing.'

I hurry out of the room, too scared to stay. I go into the kitchen. My tummy's rumbling but it seems so awful to start making tea at such a time. And half the dishes are missing. There's the teacups and saucers on the tray in the living room. I peep inside the dining room. The table is still laid. The three plates are set with luncheon meat and pickle and salad. The bread is hardening on the board. Grandad's Guinness has gone flat in his glass. His chair is lying on the floor but that is the only sign of disturbance. I don't dare touch the chair to put it to rights.

I'll have to tell Auntie Win what Nan said. I go upstairs and knock on her bedroom door. She's lying on her bed in her dressing gown.

'Auntie Win,' I say loudly, but she doesn't stir.

She's holding something large and soft in her arms. It looks almost like a teddy bear. Then I recognise the worn yellow wool. Grandad's cardigan.

# Chapter 7

I've never been to a funeral before. It's not how I expected. I thought it would be dark and dramatic, with organs and sobbing and lashing rain. It feels far too ordinary and everyday in this small crematorium, all ugly yellow wood and wilting chrysanthemums. It's almost like being in the school hall, especially now we're singing a hymn. We make such a thin reedy sound. The vicar's voice is loudest. Auntie Win and Nan are only whispering the words. Grandad's friends are silent, although they stare respectfully at their hymn book. There are just the two friends: a little grey man who used to work in Grandad's office, and a fat red man with whom he once played bowls. The only other mourner is Mrs Roberts from up the road who used to come to tea with Nan, although they've got out of the habit recently. Mrs Roberts is wearing a special black costume obviously reserved for funerals.

Our own mourning clothes are more haphazard. Nan is wearing an old black hat that's been squashed out of shape at the top of her wardrobe for years; her black cardigan cuffs show below the sleeves of her beige winter coat. Auntie Win is making do with navy, but she's carrying her big black patent handbag. I'm wearing my awful school duffle coat and my green winter frock but I've tied a black velvet ribbon in my hair. I wanted to wear black tights too, I bought a pair specially from Marks and Spencer, but Auntie Win said they looked too tarty for a girl of my age and made me wear the green woollen things that match my dress. I itch inside them, miserably apprehensive.

I look at the large casket in front of us, with Nan's wreath and Auntie Win's surprisingly showy lilies and my little posy carefully arranged on top. I can't quite grasp the fact that Grandad is inside. We are singing *Abide With Me*, his favourite hymn. He used to sing it in his bath if it was the wrong time for The Archers to keep him company. Sometimes he'd duck down and blow the tune in bubbles. I was not allowed in to see him but we'd shout silly messages through the bath-room door. Grandad would pretend to be at sea and comment on storms and shipwrecks and the occasional sighting of a mermaid, and when he came out of the bathroom, salmon pink in his clean vest and trousers, braces trailing, he'd present me with a piece of coral (a rose bath cube), a nugget of gold (Pears soap), or a bottle of finest madeira (the shampoo).

I stare at the coffin and will Grandad to shift the lid and sit up, crowned in our wreaths. Why can't he climb out and start singing along with us? I gabble a prayer to a God I haven't spoken to since primary school but noth-ing happens. Then I remember Selina and I think of the words of the Lord's prayer. Aren't witches supposed to say it backwards? I find the words in the prayer book and start at the bottom. Auntie Win is frowning at me.

'You're looking in the wrong book,' she hisses.

I take no notice. I pray backwards, clenching my fists until they tingle, biting my lips until they burn. I shut my eyes and shudder with the effort. There's a whir, a creaking. My eyes snap open in shock. *The coffin is moving!* I scream but Auntie Win has her hand over my mouth before I can draw fresh breath.

'May! Sh now! It's all right, dear. The coffin's just going out now, it's all part of the ceremony. You mustn't make a noise. Cry *quietly.*' Her own eyes are brimming.

Nan sits down, overcome, her handkerchief hiding her face. The coffin creaks on its way. It's all part of the ceremony. Nothing to do with me. Grandad glides

57

through two purple curtains. He's gone.

It's all over now, but we hover uneasily outside the chapel, no-one knowing quite what to say. Grandad's two friends mumble to Nan and then hurry away, although we expected them to come back with us for their tea. Auntie Win spent all morning making up salmon and cucumber bridge rolls and icing fairy cakes. But Mrs Roberts squashes into the funeral car with us, unasked. She talks non-stop. Nan nods every now and then but I don't think she's listening. Auntie Win makes a reasonable attempt at conversation, rubbing at her eyebrows the way she always does when she's getting a migraine.

Mrs Roberts and I are left alone together in the living room when we get back.

'Same wallpaper and curtains,' she says, looking around. 'And you still haven't had central heating put in. I don't know how you manage.' She gives an elaborate shiver although I've switched on all the bars of the electric fire and she's sitting right in front of it.

She's looking at me now.

'How old are you, May? Twelve, is it?'

'I'm nearly fifteen!'

'No! I'd never have believed it. My granddaughter's a year younger than you and yet you should see her, fancy hair, full make-up, high heels — but tasteful, mind, although they're going to have to keep an eye on her. The boys are already buzzing like bees round the honeypot.' She makes silly buzz buzz noises. 'Still, it's not your fault you look so young for your age.' She glances at the open door and lowers her voice. 'Is Nannie a bit strict with you, dear?'

I wriggle.

'It seems such a shame, a young girl like you cooped up with a lot of old folks. After all, they were all getting on a bit when your Mum arrived on the scene. Still, you're very welcome to come over to my place when my granddaughter comes visiting. She brings all her records round and does all this disco dancing for us, oh we do have a laugh. You'd really enjoy yourself, duckie.'

It is a great relief when Nan comes in with the Christmas bottle of Harvey's Bristol Cream and Auntie Win bears down on us with bridge rolls.

We eat and sip and sip and eat. Mrs Roberts carries on long after we are finished. She doesn't seem to have any intention of going home. She's edged her feet out of her hard black shoes and undone the buttons of her jacket.

'Might as well let myself spread a bit,'she says.

She seems to be spreading all over the living room, her puffy flesh rising like dough. If we're not careful we'll never be able to knead her back inside her suit and shoes. Auntie Win rather pointedly suggests a fresh pot of tea. Mrs Roberts nods happily. She starts on the bourbons and custard creams with the second pot, nibble nibble, natter natter.

Nan is going nod nod. She falls fast asleep, snoring, crumbs vibrating on her chest. Auntie Win frowns and flushes. Mrs Roberts sucks a shred of cucumber from her teeth, and they clack disapprovingly.

'It's those tranquillizers,' says Auntie Win. 'They're very strong.'

'Oh yes, dear, don't worry on my account. I quite understand. And she's getting on a bit anyway, isn't she? It's quite worn her out, poor thing. Affected her badly, I can see that. Well, it would, wouldn't it? She and Arthur being so devoted.' She smiles sweetly at Auntie Win. 'Like a pair of love-birds, those two. I remember when they first came to live here as newly weds. Of course I was only a girl then. Every morning at ten to eight you'd see them at the doorstep, Arthur giving Annie her kiss goodbye, and then at half past five every day you'd see Annie stepping out in one of her natty little outfits, off to the station to meet Arthur off the train. There go the lovebirds, that's what we'd say.' She licks pink icing from her lips, finishing up the fairy cakes. 'It's a wonder you didn't feel a bit out of it when you came to live with them, Win.'

'They made me very welcome,' Auntie Win says stiffly.

'Oh I dare say they did, but all the same … It's a pity you didn't ever find yourself a man, Win.'

'I've no complaints,' says Auntie Win. She stands up, brushing non-existent crumbs from her own clothes. It's as if she's trying to brush away Mrs Robert's sticky speech. 'If you don't mind I'll put the television on. I'd like to hear the news.'

'The news! It can't be six o'clock already,' Mrs Roberts exclaims, as she's supposed to. 'Dear oh dear, I never meant to stay so long. You must be sick of the sight of me.'

'Not at all,' says Auntie Win, not even trying to sound convincing.

Nan wakes up and blinks at Mrs Roberts in confusion. Mrs Roberts pats her cheek as if she's a baby. She spends another five minutes saying goodbye but at last she's gone.

'That woman,' says Auntie Win, fumbling in her handbag for more aspirins. 'Oh God, my head.'

'Do you want one of the doctor's pills, Winnie?' Nan asks, rubbing her eyes.

'No thanks. And you'd better not have any more either. Look at the state you're in.'

'I don't know what you mean, dear.'

'You've been snoring your head off most of the afternoon.'

'No I haven't. I wasn't asleep. I was just resting my eyes a little because they're so sore,' says Nan. 'And anyway I didn't sleep a wink last night. You've no idea what it's like in that bed. The sheets still smell of him, Win.'

'Annie,' Auntie Win says sharply.

'And I keep reaching out, thinking he's there, and I can't find him, and then I get worried something's happened to him and I tell myself not to be so silly, that it's perfectly all right, he's just got up to go to the lav, and I lie there waiting, listening, until I remember that it isn't

60

all right, it's never going to be all right again, because
—' She's crying again.

'Perhaps you'd better take another pill after all,' says
Auntie Win. 'That's it, take the pill, and then we'll tuck
you up in bed. It's the best place for you. Come on,
May, take her other arm and help me get her upstairs.'

It takes us a long time to accomplish this, and even
longer to help her get undressed. Auntie Win slips
Nan's brushed nylon nightie over her head while she's
still wearing her woollen vest and her long white bloom-
ers, preserving propriety, but I still can't bear to see her
sad old body in those silly sagging clothes. She holds
her arms up obediently for Auntie Win just like a little
girl. Auntie Win escorts her to the bathroom while I
hang around the bedroom, waiting. I turn down a
corner of the bed, and then I pull the sheets back
quickly and sniff them. She's right, they do smell faintly
of Grandad. It frightens me. I wonder about changing
the sheets for her, although the good pair of winceyette
won't be back from the laundry until Friday. Perhaps I
can make do with the summer cotton. Auntie Win
hears me rummaging in the airing cupboard and puts
her head out of the bathroom.

'Whatever are you doing, May?'

'I'm looking for clean sheets for Nan.'

'For Heaven's sake, I'm not changing that bed now.
I've got such a splitting headache I can hardly see. I
want to get Nan settled, get the place cleared up a bit,
and then get straight to bed myself. Is that too much to
ask?'

'But I thought — Nan wants clean sheets, she *said*.'

'No I don't! Leave those sheets. Leave those sheets!'
Nan calls frantically. 'What's she doing, Win? Can't you
stop her meddling?'

I go to my own room. I don't take off my clothes but
I lie down on my bed and pull the eiderdown over me. I
lie in the cold and the dark for a long time. And then
there's a knocking at the door. I won't answer. Auntie
Win comes in anyway.

61

'Are you awake, May?' She puts on the light. She sees my face before I can hide it. 'Oh *May.*'

She sits on my bed and feels for my hand.

'Poor little lovie,' she says softly, but then she feels that I'm still in my dress. 'What are you doing? Where's your nightie? Oh May, your best frock and it's getting all crushed.' She sighs heavily. 'Oh well. It's easily enough ironed. I'm sorry, dear. We've all been a bit sharp with you but it's not your fault, is it?'

It is, Auntie Win. It's my fault.

# Chapter 8

It feels as if I've been away from school for years. I can't believe it's less than a week. I feel stupidly shy as I open the door of the classroom. Most of the girls don't even look round, but Louise and Carol see me and then glance away, embarrassed. They must have heard about Grandad. Auntie Win rang the school.

'May!' Selina. She didn't come back to the house. She didn't even ring. But now she puts her arms round me. 'Poor May. I'm so sorry about your Grandad,' she says, holding me close.

I stiffen and shrug away from her softness and jasmine smell.

'Are you cross with me?' Selina whispers.

She looks prettier than ever today, her hair frizzed into a fluffy black cloud, her eyes outlined with Kohl. Her skin is white and flawless, taut over her high cheek-bones, delicately veined at her temples and eyelids.

My skin is white too but it's the sickly sort of white that often looks pale green. There are purple shadows under my eyes and eight spots on my face. One on my nose, one on my chin, two on my left cheek and four on my forehead. I have been eating sweets and endless slabs of bread and jam just for something to do. It has been so boring cooped up all week with Nan and Auntie Win. I hoped and hoped Selina would come round.

'You're cross, aren't you,' says Selina.

I try to turn away, ducking my head, but she catches

hold of me. She bends her head so she can see my face.

'Oh dear. Come on. Won't you make friends?'

'Shut up, Selina. Everyone's staring at us.'

'What do I care?'

'*I* care.'

'Yes, well, they're very sympathetic stares. Everyone's so sorry for you. And I am too.'

'You sound it.'

'I *am.*'

She's so close to me her breath tickles my face. 'Poor May,' she whispers. 'Poor little sad sister-witch.'

I remember the kiss inside the pentacle. My face burns. Selina's eyes shine.

'Why do you always get round me?' I say, pushing her away and going to my desk. I start rummaging for the day's books. 'Why didn't you come and see me?'

'Because I can't stand it when people die,' says Selina, sitting up on the neighbouring desk and stretching out her legs to admire her shapely ankles. 'I knew your Grandad was dead as soon as I saw your Auntie's face.'

'Everyone hates the idea of death,' I say crossly.

'I have this real phobia about it. Bruno once took me to this huge Victorian Cemetery at Highgate and I simply hated it. I kept thinking about all these rotting bodies right underneath my feet, thinking about bony fingers reaching out for me . . .'

'I thought I'd raised my Grandad from the dead,' I say, consulting my timetable.

'What?'

I tell her about the funeral, mimicking Auntie Win, turning it all into a pantomime. I still churn and shake when I think of Grandad, but turning it into a black comedy helps control the terror. Each sick joke and sour comment goads it further into a corner until it's down in the pit of my stomach, undetectable.

Selina seems impressed by my performance. And then the bell rings and Mrs Prendergast comes into the classroom to take the register. She pauses when she comes to me.

'It's good to see you back, May,' she says. 'How are you, dear?'

I'm astonished. Mrs Prendergast takes Maths and she's nearly always angry with me because I'm so hopeless at it. She starts off trying to explain a problem, speaking so slowly, so patiently, and I do try to understand, but the triangles on my page become weird rock formations in a moon landscape, graphs wiggle into washing lines and I mentally peg on shirts and socks and all sorts of interesting underwear, and jump when she suddenly shouts 'You're not listening, May Maddox!'

And I'm not listening now. She's said something about catching up on my classwork and borrowing someone's book and then when all the others troop off to the Art room she keeps me back and asks me if there's anything she can do. She seems disappointed by my lack of response, but she pats my shoulder briskly and tells me I can always slip back home if I feel school is too much for me. She is trying to be so kind. She doesn't realise I would sooner be anywhere else than at home.

I take my overall off my peg and hurry over to the Art room annexe. My overall is still too big for me though I've had it two years. Coarse green cotton flaps around my calves; the sleeves slip right over my knuckles. Auntie Win bought it. She said I'd grow into it but I'm still waiting. Sometimes I seem to be the Incredible Shrinking Schoolgirl, the smallest in the whole of the fourth year.

It doesn't make sense. I was so big as a baby that I couldn't get born. I had a huge head and so I stuck fast. They had to slit open my mother's stomach and yank me out sideways. When she came round from the anaesthetic they edged me into her arms. And then she started bleeding and they took me away and tucked me up into a cot and she died and I don't suppose I knew anything about it. Then. Nan and Auntie Win made sure I knew all about it later. They showed me the new

65

blue floral nightie she'd taken into hospital. They opened a locket and showed me a tiny plait of her golden hair. They even unwrapped a wad of tissue to show me one pretty pink fingernail. It's a wonder they didn't cut off her fingers too. The talented fingertips that won her all the prizes at school, the award at her art college, the fingers sketching out a brilliant future for the little golden girl — until I came along and altered everything.

I'm not much of a replacement.

I apologise to Miss Walker, the Art teacher, and sit down beside Selina. Miss Walker's brought in her collection of postcard reproductions from the National Gallery. We have to choose a card and copy it. I look for that Fragonard painting of the woman with the red ear but it's not there. Selina's chosen a Cranach painting of Venus. She's naked except for an elaborate hat, and she's got Selina's own knowing expression. She is not very good at art. She's started drawing the figure too high on her page and she's getting the proportions wrong. It's a stiff skimpy stick-woman, not Cranach's soft sexy Venus.

I flick through the postcards and find an odd portrait of a couple. They are standing holding hands, very stiff and solemn in their old-fashioned clothes. The woman is wearing a white head-dress and a long green robe; the man is clothed in black from head to foot. I settle down and dip my brush in black paint; I sketch in the outlines and then start colouring the man's clothes.

Selina peers at my painting.

'Why on earth did you pick that picture?'

'I like it.'

'It's boring. They're so ugly.'

'No, they're not.'

'Yes they are. And look at her stomach, she's pregnant.'

'She isn't. It's just the way her dress goes.'

'I can't stick this sort of painting, all fiddly and dull and old-fashioned. Why can't we have some postcards

66

of modern art? You should have seen some of the paintings in Paris. Some of them were so rude you wouldn't
believe it. And in the Beaubourg, that's where they have
all this modern art, there's an actual room you can go
in, it's just like a real bedroom only very old-fashioned.
A bit like your place, all twiddly ornaments and lacey
doilies and an old wireless. It's playing real music and
there's a couple in bed, actually having it off.'

'A real couple?'

'No, they don't go that far. Well, they couldn't keep it
up, could they? It's two weird model figures, with great
gawpy sort of heads. They gave me the creeps, actually.'

'What sort of gawpy heads?'

'Huge.'

'Bigger than mine?'

Selina bursts out laughing. Miss Walker frowns in
our direction.

'Come on, you two. Settle down. It's time you started
painting, Selina.'

Selina sighs elaborately.

'I haven't finished the drawing yet, have I?' she
announces. She stares at it. 'I can't get this stupid little
Cupid to go right, it just looks like a blob. It's a pretty
pathetic god of love if you ask me, unless you happen to
be a complete paedophile. You do its little legs for me,
May, go on.'

I lean over and sketch in a few lines, standing him on
his own two feet.

'That's better.' Selina wipes at his blobby body with
her rubber.

'You do the rest of him too, go on, May, there's a
darling.'

So I draw in a bad-tempered little baby Cupid, swot-
ting at the wasps that are attacking him. Selina draws
the wasps herself, and prints BUZZ BUZZ BUZZ in tiny
letters coming out of their mouths.

'No, don't laugh, but haven't you noticed, I've got a
bigger head than usual.'

'Well May, yes, come to think of it I had wondered

about them letting you out of the Freak show.'

'Don't.'

'Oh come on, don't be daft. Of course you haven't got a big head. Don't stop drawing the rest of his face, go on.'

'It's big compared with the rest of me. It's bigger than your head, I'm sure it is, and yet I'm much smaller than you are.'

'Oh God. You're not scared you're a midget, are you?' says Selina. She's trying not to laugh, but her mouth's quivering. 'You are a nutcase.'

'Oh finish his face yourself,' I say, and I go back to my own painting.

I did worry about being a midget once. I've always been so much smaller than everyone else. And even this Christmas, watching *The Wizard of Oz* on the television, I couldn't help wondering, and I had to stand up just to catch sight of myself in the mirror above the fireplace. If I was big enough to see myself in the mirror then of course I couldn't be a midget. Nan and Auntie Win say I'll grow soon. Grandad says it doesn't matter, I'm his favourite little tiddler. He says. Said. Oh God.

'Why's she crying, Selina?' Louise hisses. 'It's just her Grandad that's died, isn't it?'

'My Grandad died two years ago and I didn't stay off school and make such a fuss,' says Carol.

'Yes, but it's different with May. Her parents died when she was a baby. She lives with her grandparents and an old auntie.'

'Is that why she's a bit ...?'

I blow my nose and start painting, even though I can barely see. Shall I supply the word, Louise? I am a misfit.

"I suppose I've always been a bit of a misfit. I didn't fit in at school. I was too lazy for the swots, too weedy for the hearties, too timid for the trouble-makers. I didn't fit in on the estate. I wasn't tough enough to be part of any gang. I wasn't crude enough to join in the furtive sessions in the bike sheds. Yet I wasn't quite wet enough to get beaten up every time I set foot on my own back balcony. And I didn't fit in at home either. But then I didn't want to."

That's a quote from *The Misfit*. By Robin Campbell. I know that bit by heart. I've read the whole book twice, and I've read my favourite bits over and over again. It's the best book I've ever read. I wonder how much of it is true. It couldn't be all made up, it's far too real. Robin *must* be like Mark, the boy in the book.

I can't wait to see him. I feel as if I know so much about him now. Oh Robin.

I finish the man in black. I start on the woman. Only she's really very young when I look closely. Maybe only about my age. I paint her white head-dress, her green robe. Her hair barely shows. It's blonde on the postcard but I make it red. She is holding the man's hand. I paint their clasped fingers very carefully, and as I paint I say a spell inside my head.

# Chapter 9

There he is at last!

But he's not on his own. He's with a whole crowd of sixth years. They are all chatting and laughing as if they are at a party. His hand is on that blonde girl's shoulder.

I start rushing across the playground, getting away as fast as I can. I'm an idiot. He's making a fuss of everyone. He probably only said that about my writing to be kind. I don't expect he's given me a second thought. I don't suppose he even noticed I was missing on Monday. There was no point hanging around waiting for him. He won't want to be bothered reading my changeling story.

'May. May!'

I know it's him. But I don't turn round, I don't stop, I go even faster.

'*May*!'

I think he's running. He's running after me.

'Didn't you hear me talking to you?' he asks, out of breath, at my side.

He's had his hair cut even shorter. It's standing up like duckling down. It looks so silly and yet so cute. His ears look very exposed. The cold's making them go as red as his glasses.

'Where have you been? I've been looking all over for you. Where were you yesterday? We started *The Crucible* and I had a part all planned for you.'

'I was away.'

We're at the school gate. The sixth years squeeze past us, calling goodbye to him, giving him little smiles. So I say goodbye too, but he frowns at me.

'Hang about. What's been the matter with you then? A case of chronic deafness, is that it? I was yelling my head off at you just now and you wouldn't even turn round.'

'I had to go to a funeral.'

That's shut him up. He stares at me, his ears going even redder.

'Whose funeral?' he asks quietly.

'My grandfather. I lived with him.'

I told him about my mother being dead the last time I talked to him. He must think my relations are dying off like flies.

'Were you very close?'

I nod. I don't want to say any more. And he understands.

'Which way do you go home?' he asks.

I point down the road.

'That's my way too. I've got a flat near the football ground. Well, I call it a flat. The agent calls it a flatlet. It consists of three cupboards. One's called the bed-sitting room. That's an accurate description. There's only room to sit on the bed. Then there's something called a kitchenette. That contains the cooker. And then there's the shower and loo. The toilette!'

He's being so kind, giving me time to compose myself. He's so *nice*. He's just like Mark in *The Misfit*. No, he's better than Mark because he's mature. Mark was only a boy of thirteen. Robin is a man of ... thirty? I wish I knew how old he really is. Although he's too old for me. And anyway, he's married. Yes, what about his wife and his daughter? How do they fit into his little flat?

'How–how long have you been living in your flat?'

'Just a couple of weeks. I'm not sure I'm going to be able to stick it the six months I'll be here. Your school governors were supposed to fix me up with a place but

71

all they could come up with was a room in your care-taker's flat, and he didn't seem very thrilled with the idea, and I don't really blame him, so I said I'd fend for myself. It hasn't been a very auspicious start, has it? Your Miss Beecham still hasn't forgiven me for not being old Robert Campbell.'

'I did feel sorry for you then.'

'Did you?' He looks really touched. 'Never mind about being sorry for me. You're the one who's having the tough time. Tell you what. Come back to my funny flatlette and have a cup of coffee, eh?'

I blush. I can feel my face flame. I am burning right down to my breasts.

'I–I'd love to, Mr Campbell, but–but I've got to get home.'

'Oh. Yes. Okay then.'

'It's not that I don't want to or anything.'

'It's all right. I understand.'

You don't, you don't. *Shall* I go? But I can't, Nan and Auntie Win will worry so, and I'm late enough already. Although why should I always have to put them first? I've never come first with them.

'I wrote you a story.'

'Did you? Can I see it?'

'It didn't really turn out properly. It's no use, really.'

'Stop being so coy. Have you got it with you?'

'No, it's at home,' I lie. 'At least I think it is.'

I fumble in my school bag. My story is folded inside my jotter but I don't dare hand it over. I'm scared it gives too much of me away. So I leave my jotter at the bottom of my bag and pretend to search the rest of my books.

'Here's your book,' I say, bringing out *The Misfit*.

'Oh. Look, it's probably not your sort of thing at all. Please don't feel obliged to read the damn thing. It's all a bit crude and basic —'

'Now who's being coy?' I say daringly.

He smiles. I hand him his book.

'I've read it already. I've read it twice actually. I think

it's wonderful. It was so *sad* at the end — and yet I can see why it had to be like that.'

'I don't know what to say! I'm so glad you like it. You really did? I think it's my favourite out of my books and yet no-one else seems to think that much of it. There was a great fuss about it because of some of the so-called sexy bits. What did you think, May? I mean, isn't that what real thirteen year olds are like? That's what I was like anyway.'

'So is Mark you?'

'No. Well, bits I suppose. But I wasn't quite so — No, he's not me. I didn't have that sort of childhood. I didn't have to go looking for my real father. He was stuck in his armchair at home, reading the *Sporting Life*.'

'Oh. I know it's stupid but I thought it must be real.'

'Sorry. I made it all up. Oh dear, you look dis-appointed.'

'No, I'm not. It just seems so strange. I believed it and yet you made it all up, even those detailed little diary entries? What gave you the idea in the first place?'

'I don't know. I wanted to write about a thirteen year old boy and at that age you start thinking about who you are and what you're going to be and–and oh God don't I sound pompous, as if I'm giving my little lecture to schools: Why I write for teenagers. It just seemed a good idea for a story. No, that's not right either. When my own father died I suppose I felt some sort of regret because we'd never really been close, never really *said* much to each other. So I imagined what it must be like not to have ever known your father. You'd imagine so many different things about him, turn him into a fantasy figure, and then you'd want to find him so badly. Wouldn't you?'

'Well. I suppose so.'

Would I want to find my father if he were still alive? I don't think so. He didn't want me. Auntie Win said he wouldn't even take me in his arms to have a proper look at me. I don't suppose he could forgive me. He certainly didn't want to look after me. He left me with Nan and

73

sold his house and started drinking too much. Perhaps that's why he crashed the car when I was six months old. Or perhaps it was deliberate and he'd decided it was the simplest way to kill himself. Or perhaps I had grown sick of waiting for him to come and claim me and had put a hex on him.

'What would you do, May?' Robin asks.

'I don't know. I think it all depends on the father. I didn't think much of Mark's. Or his mother or his step-father, although they were quite nice to him some-times.'

'But you liked Mark himself?'

'I loved him,' I say. And blush. 'I'd better go. I'm ever so late,' I gabble and I start running.

It's all right. I saw him smile. He understands. I love *him*. I love him. Oh I love him I love him I love him.

What's the matter with me? Grandad's only just died. I can't possibly be happy. Poor Nan and Auntie Win are withering with grief. I shake my head and my hair flies wildly about my face. Nan can't be bothered to plait it for me now. I run my hand through it and hear it crackle.

I start another story on the way home.

There was once a young serving maid who lived in a frozen house. She worked hard from dawn to dusk but no matter how she toiled she shivered with bitter cold. The house was made of hard-packed snow with shining ice for windows. Icicles formed decorative chimneys and ledges and a patterned porch, but the house still seemed bleak. The ice windows did not let in much light so the rooms were dark. The little serving maid's hands ached unbearably as she swept the frosty carpets and polished the frozen furniture. She shook with the cold and even her fiery red hair could not warm her.

The chill did not seem to affect the Master and Mistress and Head Housekeeper. They went about their business briskly and never complained, so the little serving maid did not like to complain either. A pain started in her chest and grew steadily worse. She started crying and found she could not stop. The Master and Mistress and Head Housekeeper treated her kindly at first but when she started to shriek they lost patience and bundled her out of the house. The serving maid lay down in the snow, still shrieking. When the dawn came at last the pain suddenly stopped. She felt an immense explosion in her chest. She looked down and saw scarlet shards sticking out of her nightdress. Her heart had frozen fast and broken into fragments. She fingered them in astonishment. There was now such a strange hollow feel to her chest that she took a lump of coal and swallowed it. It stuck fast in the cavity and started beating of its own accord. And as it beat it sent new black blood around her body, new black thoughts into her brain. She went inside the house with a new black gleam in her eyes. Her hair crackled like fire. She was warm for the first time in her life. The snow melted wherever she took a step. There was a steady drip drip drip. The Master and the Mistress and the Head Housekeeper cowered away from the little serving maid, as if scared she might scorch them.

# Chapter 10

I shut the front door and stand in the hall. I hate the smell of our house. It's so old: old plaster, old polish, old people. I can't ever get used to it. Sometimes I can even taste it at the back of my throat.

'Cooeee. In the kitchen.'

I know. I don't want to join you. I want to run out of the house all the way to Robin's flat. I could be there with him now. I must be mad. Selina would have been off like a shot. Perhaps he'll ask her next time.

'May?' Auntie Win is at the kitchen door. 'Why are you so late, dear?'

'I'm not late.'

'Yes, you are, it's nearly quarter past. Nan and I have been on pins.'

'I keep *telling* you, we often have to stay behind a bit.'

'All right, all right. Anyway, you're here now. Come and sit down and have a cup of tea.'

Nan shuffles into view. 'Where have you been, lovie, you're ever so late,' she says, taking hold of my hand. 'Oh dear, Win, the child's frozen! Come and get warm.'

She nudges me in front of the boiler, rubbing at me feebly.

'Here dear.' Auntie Win puts the cup of tea in front of me. There's cake too, not one of the funeral fairy cakes but an iced bun bought specially from the baker's shop. I don't *want* them to be kind to me. They hover by my side, asking me questions, giving me little nods and pats, making such a fuss of me. I could almost be Amy.

'Come on, eat up that iced bun, May. I bought sausage rolls from the shop too. I thought they'd do for supper with a spot of salad. There hasn't been time for any baking — and I've still got my Head.' Auntie Win rubs it with the tips of her fingers, ruffling her eyebrows the wrong way.

'Oh dear, have you still got that headache, Win? Why don't you ask Arthur for one of his aspirins?'

We stare at Nan. I can feel myself blushing. Auntie Win is also unnerved. She starts talking about head-aches in a high-pitched voice while she washes a lettuce, shaking each leaf violently.

'It's those pills,' she mouths at me, running the cold water tap. 'She got a bit upset this morning so I gave her a couple. That's why she's–she's a bit muddled.'

'I'd better go and get on with some homework,' I say hurriedly.

'Right you are, dear. Well, I'll call you at suppertime. Here, what's that on your skirt?'

It's paint. For once my great green overall proved inadequate.

'Your good school skirt,' says Auntie Win, dabbing at it with the dishcloth. She sighs and then looks closely at the cloth. It's a shred of string vest, one of Grandad's old cast-offs. Auntie Win stops dabbing. She cups the dishcloth reverently.

'Yes, I did this watercolour in Art. It's a copy of an early Flemish painting. Jan van Eyk.' I still can't dis-tract her. 'Miss Walker seemed to think an awful lot of it.'

'Really?' Auntie Win drops the dishcloth on the draining board.

Miss Walker said I'd put a lot of thought into my painting. She didn't realise the sort of thought. And new thoughts hum in my head now like bees.

'She thinks I need some extra teaching after school,' I say casually.

'Oh? Why's that then? Haven't you been getting such good marks? I thought you came top in your last exam.'

77

'Yes, but she thinks I could still improve. Develop.'

'I see,' says Auntie Win, nodding. 'Yes. She obviously thinks you've got real potential, May. I suppose you've told her about your mother?'

'She thinks it would be good if I could stay after school sometimes and do some work with her in the art room.'

Auntie Win tweaks at my skirt and then straightens up.

'There, I think I've got it all off. It doesn't seem to show. I don't quite see why? I mean, you paint at home, don't you. Did you tell her you got your special oil paints for Christmas?'

'Yes I did, but she thinks I'd be better working with her, so she can sort of advise me, show me where I'm going wrong — and work at this special still life she's set up.'

'It still seems a bit — I mean, you've got all your homework to do and it gets dark so early. I don't like the idea of you staying behind all by yourself.'

'Oh, it's not just me. There's some other girls. It's a proper Art Club. It's mostly the fifth form though, the ones who are doing Art in their exams.'

'Oh, I *see.*'

'And if I don't go I'm scared I'll get sort of left out.'

'She'd never do that, dear, it's obvious you've inherited your mother's talent. Which day does she want you to stay behind?'

'I'm not quite sure. Maybe tomorrow. That's the trouble, I don't think it's going to be a fixed day, it's when all the others can make it. It's difficult because some of them have choir rehearsals, netball practice, that sort of thing. So couldn't I just go when everyone else does, and if I'm late home you'll know where I am, doing art. Simple.'

Of course it isn't simple. Auntie Win worries about it for ages. I tell her I'll phone her whenever I have to stay, but she still frowns and chews at her lip.

'We'll see,' she says.

I know I'm not going to get any further now so I go upstairs to my room. My mother smiles at me but her eyes are reproachful. I take the photograph and hide it behind a pile of books, but I'm so used to seeing the photograph on my desk that it still seems to be there, smiling in thin air. I get it out again and look at it. I've looked at it all my life, so many times that it's hard to see her properly. A pretty girl of my own age. That's all she is. So who cares what she thinks? I care. I can't hide her. She won't go away. Sometimes I'm scared I'll look in the mirror and find her staring back at me, and then I won't even be me any more.

I take my old box of water colours, fill a jug and balance the big photoframe on my knees. I moisten my brush and mix scarlet and yellow ochre until I have the right red. I paint flaming hair until all her gold has gone. It shines round her shocked face, a mockery of a halo. Only it's not going to be her face any more. I clean my brush and dry it and apply a thick coating of Chinese white. I don't want any of her showing through. And now the eyes, my green eyes. I'm looking at me.

I've done it. She's not there any more. I've rearranged Amy into May. I hold the frame in my hand and stare at the new technicolour photograph. I stare and stare, trying to get used to it. I can't keep it in focus. My hands start shaking. I hear Auntie Win coming up the stairs and in a panic I wet a rag and wipe the glass frame. Oh yes, I didn't dare paint the photograph itself. The paint isn't even dry. One two three wipes and it's nearly all gone. She smiles through the smears of red, smiling the way she always smiles, smiling and smiling.

> Do you know the story of the big sister and
> the little sister? Oh the big sister was so
> beautiful. She had long golden curls right
> down to her kneecaps and eyes as blue as the
> summer sky. She smiled and sang as she

79

went about her work. She painted portraits for a living. Half the village had the big sister paint their picture, and the Lord of the Manor sent for her and asked her to paint him in his splendid robes. The big sister was certainly a credit to her family. They were so very proud of her.

It was a shame about the little sister. She was small and spindly with hair the colour of the common carrot and eyes as green as duckweed. She tried to paint portraits too but she lacked her sister's skill. She scribbled and blotched as best she could but all her painted people looked like pumpkins. The family sighed and shook their heads in despair.

One day a strange girl came tripping through the village. Her face was as white as the moon, her hair as black as night. She asked the big sister to paint her portrait. The big sister used her costliest pigments and her finest brushes. The portrait was a success and the strange girl seemed delighted. She gave the big sister a bag of gold and kissed her on the lips. The big sister smiled and thanked the strange girl in her pretty way and as she spoke her honeyed words a little sticky moisture dripped from her rosy lips.

The strange girl did not ask the little sister to paint her portrait. She did not kiss her or give her a bag of gold. She did not even speak to her, although she gave her one disconcerting wink as she walked past. The little sister stared after her until she was out of sight.

The big sister smiled and smiled and every time she spoke more moisture formed at the corners of her lips and dribbled daintily down her chin. Her mother mopped the moisture, and then tasted it in wonder. It was the sweetest most delectable honey. Every time the big sister smiled, every time she spoke, the honey dribbled. It was quite an inconvenience. The big sister had to carry a little glass jar to collect the sticky golden fluid, and every morning she had to change the linen on her pillow. The big sister's mother filled jar after jar of the fabulous honey and sold it at five whole sovereigns per pot. The King himself sent for a pot and when he tasted it he said he must meet this magical girl and make her his Queen so that he could suck the sweetness straight from her lips. He sent his gold carriage for the big sister and she stepped inside, waving to her mother and her father and her little sister.

The little sister wanted to go in the King's gold carriage too but it was out of the question. So she followed on foot, running after the rapid wheels of the carriage, running until her feet were sore and bleeding. The carriage went into a dark forest and the little sister ran after it, although she knew, *everyone* knew, that the forest was a fearful place, harbouring savage bears that could kill with one claw.

She could hear the bears growling. They came padding padding through the tall trees, their eyes crazed and yellow, their noses high in the air, smelling a strange sweet scent. They smelt the little sister too, but when they saw her wild hair they cowered away from her, thinking it was fire. They smelt a far sweeter scent. The wondrous cloying golden stench of honey. They spotted the carriage. The smell grew overpowering. They tore out the horse's throat, they overturned the carriage, they felled the King's coachman, killed the King himself, and *then* they set upon the big sister. They gobbled her all up until not one golden curl was left.

The little sister watched for a while. Then she walked on by herself. And after a while she smiled.

# Chapter 11

I didn't have the nerve on Tuesday. Or Wednesday or Thursday. I couldn't make myself ask him even though I kept on bumping into him in the corridor and seeing him in the playground, and on Thursday I didn't even have to worry about slipping away from Selina because she stayed at home with a sore throat. I even walked across the playground after school with Robin, but I couldn't get the words out although they clamoured in my head like cymbals. I didn't dare say it. I was too scared. I'd constructed my elaborate alibi for nothing.

No, I'm *going* to do it today. Selina's away again. I know I'll never have a better chance. I've spent the whole day whispering the words, ready for when the bell goes.

The bell goes. It sounds inside my head as well as out. I'm going to do it now. I've got to say it now.

But where is he? He's not in the library, he's not in any of the form rooms. Is he in the playground already? No, there's no sign of him. I wait ten minutes, ten endless minutes. Nearly everyone else has gone home now. He must have gone home too. He must have slipped out before the bell. I've missed him.

I might as well give up and go home. It's all my own stupid fault. I've funked it three days running and now I've missed my chance.

I'm halfway up the road when I just happen to look round — and I spot his red scarf back at the school gate. He's waving. I wait.

'Hello, May. I hoped I'd see you. I'm a bit late, I've been closeted with your headmistress. Phew! She makes me feel as if I'm still in short trousers. Have you got the story handy? I really do want to read it.'

I open my mouth. My throat feels as if it's been stitched up.

'Yes, I've got it. And some others too.' My voice sounds strange, a silly squeak. And I'm blushing, my face burns, my temples pound, it's a wonder blood doesn't start spouting straight out my ears. It's now or never.

'Perhaps. Perhaps I could show you? Back at your flat?' I squeak in short bursts until I run out of voice altogether.

'Sure,' he says, smiling.

It's all so simple, so easy, so casual, I can't believe it.

'Would you mind if I just phone my great-aunt first? To let her know I'll be a bit late.'

'Oh you sweet considerate girl,' he says, stopping at the phone box.

He's teasing me — and no wonder. I feel idiotic shutting myself in the phone box and babbling away to Auntie Win. She keeps asking me questions and giving me advice until the pips start.

'I'll have to go. Bye, Auntie.' I put the phone down on her, though she's commanding me to put in another coin. I come out of the phone box and smile at Robin apologetically.

'Sorry about that. It's just she gets in a bit of a flap if —'

'Of course.'

We walk along together. I wish I didn't feel so stiff and self-conscious. He offers to carry my heavy schoolbag but I hang on to it, not wanting to be a nuisance. Although will he think me rude for refusing? He takes hold of my elbow and I jump. It's just because we're crossing the road, it's the gentlest of touches, purely protective, so why am I acting as if his fingers are fire? He takes his hand away the moment we're back on the

84

pavement. Oh God, I'm so stupid. Perhaps he thinks *I* think he was making some sort of pass at me. How can I explain it was just nerves? He'll think me such an idiot. I *am* an idiot. He's asking me about my family now, exactly who do I live with, the same old teacher's talk, but okay, at least it's something to talk about. Why is it so hard now? It's always been so easy before. Why do I feel so *shy*? I start the sad saga, dead mother, dead father, and now it's dead Grandad too but don't go into that, stick with Nan and Auntie Win. He's looking so concerned I can't help laying it on with a trowel. I dig dig dig at Nan and Auntie Win, emphasising their oddness, their oldness, deliberately turning them into comic cut-out crones. I shouldn't talk about them like that. It's tempting fate. Look what happened to Grandad.

'May?'

I think my face has screwed up. I ease it back into an ordinary expression.

'Sorry.'

'*I'm* sorry. Is it your grandfather?'

'Mm.'

'I don't know what to say. Perhaps I ought to shut up altogether. It sounds so stupid just keeping on saying I'm sorry.'

'It doesn't sound stupid.'

'I know I shouldn't have kept asking you all those questions but I wanted to know all about you.'

There's a little pause. I'm so pleased. I want to know all about him. Tell me about your wife, Robin Campbell. Will she be there when we get to your flat? Even though it's only a flatlet. Perhaps she's a very little unobtrusive wife. A wifelet who cooks dainty dishes in the kitchenette and then tucks herself up inside a folding bed. Although no wife could be smaller than me.

'Here we are. It's the house with the broken door and graffiti on the walls. SQUATERS RULE! The silly idiots can't even spell it right.'

'You've got squatters in your house?'

'They're just on one floor. They're perfectly harmless.

85

They decorate the walls with their spray cans and look how carefully they've planted the garden with crisp packets and Kentucky chicken cartons.'

'Very chic.' I go in the gate and step over a couple of coke cans. 'I like the three-dimensional crazy paving.'

He laughs loudly although it's not that funny. Fancy me making him laugh. The hall smells of stale chip pans and old gas cookers. Robin sniffs and smiles apologetically. It's so dark I can hardly see him.

'I'm afraid it's upstairs. Two lots of upstairs.'

His arm wavers near mine but he doesn't take hold of my elbow this time. It's my fault for being so stupid before. I watch him as he runs up the stairs in front of me. He's not quite so quick the second lot of stairs. He's panting and when he sees I've noticed he hams it up, pretending to be gasping.

'Serve me right for showing off. It's no use trying to kid myself I'm still a spry young lad.'

'You're still young,' I say seriously.

'How old do you think I am them?'

I hesitate.

'Twenty ... eight?'

'You are sweet,' he says, unlocking his door. He beckons and I step in under his arm.

'Aren't you little!'

He sees me wince.

'I think it's lovely that you're so tiny. You're the only girl who's ever made me feel tall.'

'How tall are you? Five foot six?' I'm watching his face. '. . . and a half.'

'Absolutely spot on. You're much better at heights than ages. Or were you just exercising an incredible tact when you said I was twenty eight?'

'How old are you then?'

'Thirty four.'

'You're not!'

'See, I am old.'

'No, no you're not. Well you don't look it.'

'I've got a daughter your age, remember?'

So where is she? And where is his wife? They can't live here. It's not at all how I imagined. I thought he'd have an old desk, masses of books, leather armchairs, fine prints on the walls, ethnic rugs and cushions adding decorative splashes of colour.

This room doesn't need splashes of colour. It has already drowned in it. The walls are red flock. The ceiling is purple. The formica table top is orange. There is a hilarious standard lamp with a purple plastic shade spotted with red and orange — colour co-ordination with nobs on.

'I know,' says Robin, although I haven't said a word. 'I spent the first week wearing sunglasses.'

'It's–it's very —'

'It's hideous,' Robin says. 'It's rented along with the rooms.' He goes into his kitchenette to plug in the kettle. It is orange too, with lime green cupboards. I stand in the doorway. There's a bowl of half eaten muesli and a scummy mug of coffee abandoned on the draining board.

'I got up late,' says Robin, running them under the tap.

One bowl, one mug. No wifelet. No daughterette. I wander back into the main room and examine the ornaments on his window sill: a sickly green rabbit, a cross-eyed fawn and a little brass boy with a corkscrew spiralling from his penis.

'Aren't they wonderful?' Robin calls from the kitchen. 'And you should see the pair of plaster ladies in the bedroom — I'm finding them increasingly disconcerting. I put my socks over their heads when I get undressed to stop them staring at me. Biscuit? Or there's some very elderly chocolate log. It's convincingly log-like now, if nothing else.'

'Biscuit, please.'

'Very wise. Do you want to put a tape on? They're over on the shelf.'

At last I find part of the room that belongs to Robin. There are his tapes, Dory Previn and John Lennon and some jazz and cheap classics. I stick on a symphony to make him think I'm cultured. There's a pile of books too, Penguins and Picadors and a handful of old children's books, *Bevis* and *Tom Sawyer*, Edward Lear and E. Nesbit and a fat volume of Grimm's *Household Tales*. I pick it up and flip through it.

*The Changeling.* It's only a page long, I read it in a minute.

'What are you reading?' asks Robin, coming in with a tray of coffee and a plate of munchmallows.

'Oh, it's just this fairy story. It's about a changeling. I–I wrote about a changeling too. It's not the same as the proper story though.'

'Can I see it? And any of the others that you've done?'

I hand them all over, going hot. I'm so scared he'll laugh at them and think them stupid. I stand by his shelves, sipping my coffee, waiting. He sits in the black plastic swivel armchair, reading, eating one munchmallow after another. He eats them like a little boy, nibbling the chocolate topping off first, gnawing the biscuit, then sucking the sticky mallow into his mouth. He absent-mindedly offers me the plate but I don't feel like eating at the moment. Or drinking. It's starting to be an effort breathing. *What does he think of them?*

He looks up at me at last.

'I think they're wonderful.'

It's exactly what I wanted him to say but I can't believe he means it. He's just being kind and encouraging and anyway what does wonderful mean? Wonderful for a schoolgirl but only passable for anyone else. And wonderful is an ambiguous word anyway. Perhaps he's simply full of wonder that I write such weird stuff.

He's talking about them, commenting on bits and pieces, making some tactful suggestions, but I can't take any of it in.

'Do you really think they're wonderful?'

He laughs at me.

'You're hopeless. You'll write some more, won't you?'

'If you want me to.'

'You never know, you might even get them published one day. Fairy stories go down very well at the moment. You could try and write some fiercely feminist ones with big bold peasant lasses setting out to seek their fortune.'

'I'm not very good at writing about big bold people.'

'Neither am I,' says Robin. 'I'm writing a book at the moment about a boy who's secretly in love with a girl and yet he's hopeless, he doesn't even dare speak to her.'

'Can I read a bit?'

'No.'

'That's not fair. You've read my stories.'

'They're finished. When my book's finished you can read it, okay?'

I nod and take a teacake after all.

'I'm wondering about changing tack though. I really ought to write a girl's school story now I'm doing this Writer in Residence here. You know, all Angela Brazil, jolly hockeysticks and cocoa in the common room.'

'We're not like that.'

'Oh May, look at you! White blouse and school tie and grey pleats and a *plait*.'

I burn.

'I know I look pathetic,' I mumble.

'I think you look sweet,' says Rob.

I'm not sure it's exactly a compliment. It's too sticky and sugary a word, like the cake in my mouth. But oh how I savour it all the same.

# Chapter 12

'It's for you, May,' Auntie Win announces, holding out the telephone.

No-one ever phones me up. It can't be Robin, can it? Oh God, what am I going to say to him, what will Auntie Win say, what am I going to do?

'Who is it?' I mouth at Auntie Win.

'It's Selina,' says Auntie Win, surprised that I can't work it out for myself.

'Well, you're a fine friend, I must say,' Selina croaks angrily down the phone.

'Why? What have I done?' I ask, starting to worry.

'You haven't done anything, that's the point! Here's me, stuck in bed with this foul flu or whatever it is and you haven't even bothered to phone me up to see whether I've actually sneezed myself into a stupor, let alone come round here with grapes and glossy magazines.'

'I'm sorry, I just — Look, you didn't come round last week when —'

'That was different. You weren't *ill*. And anyway you had your grandma and your aunt. I'm languishing here *alone*, I hope you realise. Well, except for Mrs Henry, but she's such a pain I'd be better off without her. Do you know her idea of invalid food? Wait for it! Cold rice pudding out of a tin. Did you ever? Who in their right mind could eat one spoonful of something that looks like bleached sick? Oh, and a bottle of Lucozade — and we all know what that looks like. So come and minister to my every need, there's a pal.'

'You mean come round this afternoon?'

'No, come and stay the weekend, eh?'

'I can't.'

'Oh don't be so hateful. *Please.* I tell you, I'm all on my own. My Dad's in America on business at the moment and my charming mother has gone off to some awful occult conference in Wales of all places. So you've got to come, May, I *need* you.'

'I can't, you know I'm not allowed.'

'Can't you just ask your aunt? She heard for herself, my voice has all gone funny with this bloody sore throat. Of course she'll let you come. I thought she was supposed to like me? Ask her, go on.'

So I put the phone down and go and ask Auntie Win. I know it's a waste of time. I don't really want to go that much anyway. I want to go to the library this afternoon to look for the rest of Robin's books. And I want to start a new fairy story. This one's going to be different. It might even have a happily ever after ending. The last thing I want to do is go and act as Selina's serving maid. I bet she's not properly ill at all. She's just got a cold and is making a fuss.

I ask Auntie Win all the same and of course she insists it's out of the question.

'I've never heard anything so silly! We don't want you going down with flu. You've been looking very peaky lately as it is.'

I'm happy enough with that, but I think I'll have to offer to go round this afternoon.

'Just to see how she is, Auntie. She's all on her own and —'

'I can't help that. I think it's disgraceful of her parents. I've a good mind to report it to someone, leaving a child that age — and ill too! Anyway, you're not going and that's that.'

I look at Nan. She is sitting on the stool at the sink, peeling potatoes. She is concentrating so hard on the skin and the knife and her two shaking hands that she obviously hasn't taken in a word of what we've been saying. There's no point going through it all over again anyway. I know exactly what she'll say. 'Do as Auntie says, there's a dear.' So I do.

'I'm ever so sorry Selina, but —'

'Oh God. I might have known.'

'Look, I can't help it, you know what they're like.'

'I know what *you're* like. A great big useless baby. All right, don't come then — even though I thought we were supposed to be best friends.'

'We are, it's just —'

'Oh no we're not. Not any more. I'm sick of you. Bloody sick, do you hear?'

She slams the phone down. I tell myself I don't care. It's not my fault anyway. And now that I've got Robin I don't really need Selina for my friend.

Only I can't go round with him at school. What am I going to do if Selina starts being really spiteful to me, the way she used to be? She knows so much more about me now, all sorts of secrets. And she'll get Louise and Carol and all the others on her side. I won't have anyone. It'll be just like in the third year. Worse.

Well I don't care.

Yes I do, I care, I care, I care.

'What are you doing, dear?' Auntie Win calls. 'Can you come and lay the table for lunch?'

I stalk into the kitchen and start laying the table, slamming down the knives and forks, dealing out the plates as carelessly as I dare. We haven't dined in the dining room since Grandad died. We don't even sit in the sitting room very often. We just crouch in the kitchen. It's got its own horrible stale smell, sad and senile. I think I'm starting to smell of it too. I lift my arm and sniff at my sleeve. I'm sure it smells. Soon it'll be in my hair, my skin.

'What ever's the matter, May? Why are you pulling that silly face? And watch what you're doing with those plates, they're not made of cast iron,' Auntie Win says sharply.

'There's a funny smell in here.'

'What smell?' says Nan, looking bewildered.

'I can't smell anything,' says Auntie Win, sniffing. Her nostrils twitch. 'What sort of smell?'

'Just a *smell* smell.'

'You're just being silly,' says Auntie Win.

I feel like being silly.

'I want to go and stay with Selina,' I say.

Auntie Win sighs impatiently.

'Don't start that again, please.'

'I don't see why I can't. I'm the only girl in my class who's not allowed to stay the night with a friend.'

'Will you be quiet, May?'

'*No!*'

There is a shocked silence in the kitchen. Nan tries to go on peeling but she drops her potato. It rolls across the lino, gathering dust.

'You musn't talk to Auntie like that,' she says, tutting.

'You're to go up to your room this minute,' says Auntie Win.

'It's not my room. It's my mother's. It's got all her things, not mine, and I'm sick of it,' I say. 'I'm sick of you too. I'm going to Selina's and you can't stop me.'

'How dare you behave like this!' Auntie Win says, outraged.

'How dare you boss me about and treat me like a baby when you're just an old great aunt, nothing to *do* with me.'

'You stupid little girl!' Auntie Win shouts. 'You think you're so clever. You don't know the half of it, Madam. I've a good mind to —'

'Win!' Nan clutches at her, still waving the potato knife.

I turn my back on their comic grappling. I run out of the kitchen, snatch my coat from the hall and open the front door. I'm out in the street before they've realised what I'm up to. I've done it! I feel as if I'm taking great strides in seven league boots.

There were once two ugly old women who lived in a crumbling cottage in the country. They were getting too old to cope and lived in terror of the Workhouse. One day they were out digging in their vegetable patch when they heard an odd little cry coming from the spindly carrots. One old woman bent down as far as her bad back would allow.

'Sister! Heaven be praised. There is a tiny tiny child amongst the carrots!' she exclaimed, and she caught the creature in her shaky old hand.

'Look at it. Did you ever see such a little oddity?'

The child was only six inches tall, with eyes as green as the gooseberries on the bush and long hair the colour of the carrots.

'She might be a fairy!'

'Then don't let her escape.'

The old woman clutched the tiny child so tightly that she cried.

'Sh!' said the old woman, shaking her like a salt cellar. 'Don't you dare make that noise. You're to do what we say, do you hear?'

They waddled indoors and put the tiny child in the biscuit tin for safe keeping. The child beat her tiny hands on the inside of the tin.

'You can drum until your hands fall off,' cackled the old woman. 'You're at our mercy now. We want fairy wishes, don't we, sister? What shall we have for the first wish, eh? I think I'd like a new silk gown.'

'And I wouldn't say no to a pair of satin slippers,' said the other old woman. 'Size 5½, wide fitting, if you please.'

They sat back expectantly but there wasn't a silk gown or satin slipper in sight.

They frowned and peeped inside the biscuit tin. The child was crouching on a custard cream, crying.

'Don't cry, you'll make the biscuits soggy. Come along, grant our wishes at once. What's the matter with you? You're not much use for a fairy. Or aren't you a fairy after all? You're not very pretty, are you? And you haven't got wings and a wand. Call you a fairy!'

'Oh dear, I could so do with a pair of satin slippers,' said the other old woman. 'Shall we take it back to the carrot patch and set it free, sister?'

But they decided to keep the tiny child in the tin just in case she should come in useful. She started growing rapidly on her diet of custard creams and bourbon biscuits. She soon found the tin a tight fit. They tried her out in the wastepaper basket and eventually kept the child in the cupboard under the stairs with all the brooms and brushes. They tied her on a long lead and once a day let her out of the cupboard to do all the cleaning. And all the washing and ironing. And then they made her cook the vegetable stew for supper. She might not be a fairy but she came in handy as a servant and they didn't even have to pay her any wages.

The child grew white and weak and spent most of her time in the broom cupboard sleeping although it was hard to clear herself sufficient space to curl up properly. She scrabbled about the cupboard and found, right at the back, a strange pair of black buckled shoes. She slipped one on her left foot, and one on her right. They fitted perfectly. Her green eyes glowed in the dark.

When the old women opened the

95

cupboard door in the morning the child stepped out in her new black buckled shoes. They grew larger and larger in the daylight, and the child grew with them. Soon she was towering above the two old women, her head pressed up against the ceiling. She lifted her left foot and stamped hard on one old woman. Then she lifted her right foot and stamped hard on the other. Then she marched out of the cottage in her great black buckled shoes, left right, left right — and she never went back.

# Chapter 13

'Selina?'

Why doesn't she answer the door? She can't have gone out, not if she's got flu. Perhaps she's really ill and she can't even get out of bed. I crouch down and peer through the letterbox. What do I expect to see? Selina crawling across the snowy carpet, fevered and fainting? The hall is silent and empty.

'Selina!' I hiss into the letter-box. 'Selina, are you all right? It's me, May. Selina, please come.'

I wait. Is that a door opening somewhere upstairs?

'*Selina*!'

'For God's sake, I'm coming. Give me a chance.'

I see her bare feet pattering down the stairs, then her white nightdress, then her long black hair. She's frowning. I snap the letter-box shut quickly and wait for her to open the door.

'What do you want?'

I stare at her.

'I've come to see you! You asked me to. I thought you wanted —'

'I thought I told you to get lost.' She coughs irritably. 'It's freezing. I'm going to get double pneumonia if I hang about on the doorstep any longer. So come *in*.'

I do as she tells me. I seem to have shrunk right back into little mouse May.

'I don't know why you're being so horrid to me,' I whine. 'I had an awful row with my aunt about you.'

'Look, I don't care about your loony old aunties. I

wish you'd shut up, I've got such a headache. I feel awful,' Selina says, rubbing her eyes.

She looks awful, almost ugly. Her hair needs washing, her eyes are puffy and her nose needs blowing. I think I woke her up because she smells of sleep. How can I stay scared of her now?

'Come on, I'll help you back to bed. Where's Mrs Henry?'

'I told her to sod off. So she did.'

'You're in a charming mood, aren't you? Well, you'd better try and be a bit sweeter to me, because it looks as if I'm the only mug left to run round after you.'

'You said you couldn't come,' Selina grumbles, clinging to me as we climb the stairs.

'Well, never mind, I'm here now.'

'And can you stay?'

'No. But I'm going to.'

'Till tomorrow?'

'Yes,' I say boldly.

'So I take it there will be dawn raids, sirens, searchlights, great posses of pigs and a pair of dotty old ladies desperate to find their mimsie little May?'

'Undoubtedly. Still, it'll amuse your neighbours if nothing else, won't it?'

Selina giggles and then suddenly reaches out and gives me a hug.

'Thanks for coming.'

'Careful, you'll topple us both down the stairs,' I say briskly.

'Excuse my display of emotion, I must be feverish,' says Selina. 'I *am*. Feel my forehead, May. It's burning.'

'Have you taken your temperature?'

'You're the one who's playing Florence Nightingale, that's your job. And I'd like my bed made, please, with a hot water bottle, and —'

'You should have hung on to Mrs Henry. And there's no point having clean sheets when you're all sweaty.'

'Sorry. I suppose I am in a pretty disgusting state,' says Selina, panting up the last few stairs. 'Oh God, I feel as if I'm going to die. My heart!'

'Please don't. I couldn't take another funeral.'

'Well, where are my grapes and magazines?' Selina demands, feeling in my coat pockets.

I gently slap her hands away.

'I've brought myself, what more do you want?'

'You haven't bought me anything, you mean pig?' Selina asks, sounding genuinely indignant.

'I haven't got any *money*.'

'Oh no, don't start all that niminy piminy poor little orphan Annie twaddle — and stop slapping me, you're hurting, and I'm *ill*.'

'Get into bed then. And don't breathe all over me, I don't want your cold.'

'It's not a cold. It's flu. Pneumonia. Double pneumonia. If not triple.'

'Trust you to think you've got three lungs. No wonder you're so lousy at biology.'

I help her into her room. The curtains are drawn but she winces when I switch on the light.

'Don't. My eyes hurt and I've got a headache.'

'All right, all right. Light off. I don't particularly want to see all your dirty knickers and tights all over the floor anyway. You are a slut.'

'It's Mrs Henry's fault, it's her job to clear up my room,' says Selina, flopping into her unmade bed.

'Hang on, I'll smooth it all for you. Come on, out the way.'

'I'm ill. I just want to lie down. I'm in pain —'

'You're the pain. Honestly! Shut up or I'll walk right out on you,' I say, smoothing sheets and plumping pillows.

'No you won't. You're staying now, aren't you.'

'Maybe.' I shake out the duvet. 'There you are, you can get in now. Do you really want a hot water bottle?'

'Please. And a hot drink too.'

'What do you want?'

'Anything. Just something hot and soothing. My throat feels as if it's been scraped with a knife.'

'It's all those sharp things you keep saying.'

'Oh ha ha. You sound just like your old auntie and nannie.'

'Don't keep on about them.'

'Did they really get in a state about you coming here?'

'Of course they did. But I don't want to talk about it. I'll go and get your bottle and drink, right?'

'So why did you come?'

I shrug. 'Goodness knows.'

'It's my fatal charm,' says Selina, turning onto her side and smiling up at me.

'Kid yourself. Take a look in the mirror. Your nose needs blowing.'

Selina laughs and wipes it on a corner of the sheet.

'Do you have to?'

'Perhaps I worked a charm. A spell. A love potion,' Selina whispers, her eyes glittering.

I stare at her, my mouth going dry.

'Haven't you ever wondered at the way I can get people to do things?' she says, tucking her tangled hair behind her ears. Her face is a pale moon in the darkened room.

'Selina — *is* it a game? Are you a witch? Am I a witch now? Tell me.'

'I thought you were going to make me that drink? Please. My throat hurts so badly,' she says, holding her throat with her long white fingers.

'Selina —'

'My God, I've got lumps!' she says, sitting up. She feels under her ears. 'May, look. Bloody great lumps.'

I look as she holds back her hair. She really has got lumps: her neck is badly swollen, especially on the left.

'I think it's your glands, yes it must be,' I say, touching them gingerly.

She winces.

'They're so sore, May. You don't think I've got something really dreadful, do you?'

'Triple pneumonia?'

'Don't joke now, I'm scared.'

'Do you want me to phone your doctor?'

'We haven't really got one. Dad sees a specialist and my mother goes to this nature cure creep. I'm certainly not calling him, he'd dose me up with deadly night-shade quick as a flash.'

'I suppose I could phone my doctor?'

'No, don't bother. I'll be okay. You're right, it is just swollen glands. I hope it isn't mumps. God, it's just as well Bruno's at Warwick, I wouldn't want to impair his potency.' She coughs again.

'I'll make you the drink.'

It takes me a long time to master the kitchen cooker. It bears no resemblance whatsoever to our stove at home, a simple upright affair, with an oven in its belly and four burners on top. This is more like a spaceship than a kitchen and it's a struggle working out which set of controls comprises the cooker. The dishwasher confuses me momentarily but at last I work it out. I fiddle with various knobs until one of the electric rings starts reddening and then I pick up the strange kettle on one of the gleaming work surfaces. I put it on the ring and wait, watching it anxiously. The metal starts to mumble to itself. I have a feeling something is wrong. Then I notice the prongs on the back of the kettle and connect them in my mind with the plug on the kitchen top. I snatch the kettle off the burner and stare at it in terror. It smells of singed metal. I stand helplessly with it hanging from my hand. I'm sure I've broken it and maybe even ruined the burner too — but when I eventually dare plug it in it actually works.

I find a couple of beautiful earthenware mugs easily enough but it's a long hard hunt for a hot water bottle. I can't find an ordinary rubber one at all but amongst a cupboard of assorted ginger jars and Clarice Cliff crockery I find a china 'hot pig' just like the one Nan uses. Selina's mother probably bought it in an antique market as an amusing kitchen decoration but I don't suppose it will do it any harm if I use it properly.

I want to make Selina a hot lemon drink, but I can't find any lemons, not even a plastic Jiff, so she'll have to have Gold Blend because that's the only beverage I can find. I wonder if she's hungry as well as thirsty. I try the fridge but a very large cheese seems to have taken it over. There are all sorts of tins in the larder but none of them seem suitable. They are either very expensive: caviar, Chinese fruit, chestnut puree — or very cheap and cheerful: baked beans, spaghetti and the spurned rice pudding. I find some stale jam sandwich biscuits in a tin and decide we'd better lunch on these. There's very little jam in the biscuit sandwich so I dare open a jar of special strawberry conserve and spoon it on liberally over the biscuits I've arranged on the plate.

I feel quite pleased with myself as I carry the jammy biscuits, coffee and the hot pig upstairs on the tray. Selina is asleep when I come into the room, breathing heavily through her mouth, almost snoring. She's very flushed and I can see little beads of sweat on her forehead. She is really ill. Perhaps I ought to call our doctor, any doctor. I put the tray down and touch her forehead very lightly.

'Mm. What a lovely cold hand,' Selina mumbles.

'You're burning.'

'I know. Don't take your hand away. That's so nice.' She flops against me and then opens her eyes properly. 'What on earth is that brown object on the tray?'

'A hot pig.'

'What am I meant to do with it? Eat it?'

'It's instead of a hot water bottle, I couldn't find one.'

'Well, *I'm* instead of a hot water bottle. I bet I'm much hotter than your hot pig. Pass me my coffee.'

'And there's biscuits. I put extra jam on, I hope it's all right. And if you're hungry there's lots of tinned stuff, I could heat something.'

'No thanks. I hate all that muck. My father spends a fortune in Fortnums and Mrs Henry buys what she calls The Basics down at Tesco's and I can't stand any of it.'

'Doesn't your mother go shopping?'

'You must be joking. She doesn't need to. She lives on Boots diet chocolate and black coffee. She's mad, she doesn't eat anything else. Just chomp chomp at a bar of methyl cellulose.'

'Perhaps that's sent her mad. It's infiltrated her blood stream and all her corpuscles have turned into cotton wool,' I suggest, licking strawberry jam.

Selina laughs.

'Does she *really* practice witchcraft?'

'I *told* you.'

'Yes, but you tell me lots of things and half the time you're teasing me.'

'Me?' says Selina, sipping coffee. She doesn't seem interested in the biscuits but I think they're delicious.

'Yes, you. Look, does your mother really believe in witchcraft? Do you?'

'Do *you*?' says Selina, handing me her coffee cup. 'I don't really want any more, sorry. Do you mind if I lie down again? I really do feel bloody.'

'Of course I don't mind.'

I tuck her up carefully and smooth her hair out of her face. The swelling on her neck looks so painful.

'You poor old thing,' I whisper, stroking her shoulder.

'Mm. I know,' Selina murmurs, closing her eyes. 'I think I might have another nap. Is that okay?'

She's asleep before I can answer. I sit by her side for a while, still stroking her shoulder, but after five minutes this becomes so boring that I ease myself up and away. I'm still ravenous so I finish up all the biscuits on the plate, even licking it for crumbs and stray smears of jam. Then I slip downstairs to the kitchen, make myself another coffee — there are ugly streaks on the base of the kettle and up one side, oh God — and I help myself to a stale end of sliced bread at the bottom of an earthenware crock. The butter in the fridge smells so strongly of cheese that I spread it with strawberry jam instead. Two layers. I shall end up

103

with spots the size of strawberries if I go on like this. I don't care. I even take a spoon and eat straight out of the jar. When I start to feel slightly sick I wander into the living room but I find the white overwhelming. There's a white marble statue of a cherub where the Christmas tree stood. At least I think it's a cherub. It has an unpleasant leer on its face. Its blank white eyes watch me until I blunder back out of the room.

I creep back to Selina. She's still fast asleep. She's breathing quite peacefully now and she doesn't look so flushed. I hope she's getting better — although the swelling stands out on her thin white neck. I sit in the chair at the dressing table. I watch her for a little while and then I swivel round and watch myself. I try out various sophisticated hairstyles, using Selina's beautiful old silver hairbrush, but my face underneath stays obstinately childish. I open her black box of make-up. It's like an artist's palette of paints. I crayon on new big brown eyes, two rosy cheeks and a sweet sugar-pink smile but I still look the same ugly old me underneath the mask of colour. I take a tissue and start wiping, peering into the mirror. I see my eyes and cheeks and lips smear into a sad blur and I suddenly panic. A sour slime of jam rises at the back of my throat. I blink wildly, unable to see for a moment, terrified that I've wiped off half my face and left an empty egg in its place — but it's still there, I'm still here, and I'm not going to think about him now, it wasn't my fault, it couldn't possibly be my fault.

I shake my head, wishing I could wipe away all my thoughts as easily as the make-up on my face. I look round Selina's room for something to read but she doesn't go in for books. I find several glossy magazines but they're nearly all pictures and the pages make such a crackle when I turn them that I'm scared I'll wake her up.

I look across at her again. She looks so peaceful now. I smile at her properly. I'd never dare smile this way if she were awake. I'm still a bit scared of her even now. I never know when she's going to start teasing. I can't ever trust her.

But she can't trust me either. What if she found out about Robin and me! What would she say if she knew I'd been to his flat? She'd never believe it. I still can't believe it myself.

'I love Robin Campbell,' I whisper, looking straight at Selina. 'And he loves me too. He does. I know he does. He's secretly in love with me but he doesn't dare say so. But I'm going to make him say it. I'm going to make him.'

Selina smiles in her sleep.

# Chapter 14

'I feel much better,' Selina says, sitting up in bed.

I sit up too and rub my eyes. I must have fallen asleep. It's starting to get dark already.

'God, what a pair of dozies!' says Selina, stretching 'I think I'll have a bath. And something to eat, I'm starving.' She reaches out for the plate of biscuits and laughs. 'You little pig.'

'I'll get you something else. Although I'm not quite sure what.'

'You be an angel, May, and go and buy something nice. You'd better get stuff for tomorrow too. There's meat in the freezer but I'm sure it's been there years. It's probably frozen dinasour fetlock and boil-in-the-bag brontosaurus. So will you go, May?'

'You'll have to give me some money.'

'Here.' She tosses me her beautiful big black leather bag.

'What shall I get?'

'Oh, anything. Use your imagination.'

'You might regret that. My imagination runs wild.'

'All the better. I like being surprised.'

So I set off for the shops, Selina's bag swinging from my shoulder. I borrow her scarf and gloves because I was in such a hurry to get out of my house I forgot my own. I wear her purple leather boots too. I didn't forget my shoes. I just love her boots. They are at least two sizes too big for me, so that my feet go for an extra little walk inside them every step I take, but I don't care. I'd wear them if the soles were sprinkled with tintacks. The boots make such a difference to my legs. They're not such silly schoolgirl legs any more. They seem proper curvy girl's legs, almost the same as Selina's. I feel like a little scale model of Selina. I can manage her walk now I'm in her magic boots, though I have to shuffle a bit to stop the boots slipping sideways. I fling my scarf over my shoulder in a careless Selina gesture, I flex my woolly fingers jauntily, I smile and swing my bag backwards and forwards, backwards and forwards, oh God, isn't that Mrs Roberts over the road, my smile stiffens, backwards, backwards —'

'May! Cooeee, May! Hello dear. Isn't it parky?'

She is wearing a black and white imitation fur coat like a dalmation and a black woolly turban hat crammed over her ears to keep out the cold.

'What are you doing up at this end of the town, eh?'

'I'm seeing a friend.'

'*Are* you! That's nice to hear. I've been a bit worried about you, cooped up in that house with your Nan not quite herself. It's really aged her, hasn't it. Made her a bit ... She is under the doctor, isn't she?'

'Oh yes, she —'

'Good. And then there's your Auntie. Well, Great Auntie, isn't she. How is she coping?'

'Oh, she's–she's all right.'

'I expect she took it very bad. She always did seem so fond of your Grandad, like. Yes, it's always tickled me, that little threesome of theirs. Well, foursome it was, with your Mum. Oh dear, what a lovely girl she was. The golden girl, that's what we all called her in the road. She was like a little Shirley Temple as a kiddie, all charm and curly hair, and she grew up into such a beautiful bobby-dazzler, and yet it didn't turn her head, she always had such a nice way with her. "Oh hello, Mrs Roberts!" I can remember just the way she used to say it.'

'I–I've got to —'

'What a pity you never knew her, dear. It seems such

107

a tragedy, never knowing your own mother.'

'I think the shops will be closing soon, and I've go to —'

'You're starting to look a bit like her, you know, now you're growing up.'

I stare at her, silenced.

'Yes, there's definitely a likeness. Of course, your hair's so red, and you're still a little shrimp of a thing, but — You do get enough to eat, don't you?'

'Of course I do!'

'Well, I know there was a lovely spread the other day, after the funeral, but I just wondered if that was, well, *usual.* Old folk don't have much of an appetite, I know, and your Auntie and Nannie just pecked at their food like sparrows.'

'They were upset.'

'Well, of course. I didn't mean — I'm not suggesting anything nasty, dear. I know they both take really good care of you, but they *are* are getting very old and your Nannie especially isn't quite what she was in the brain-box department, if you get my meaning.'

I don't want to get her meaning. I want to take off Mrs Robert's silly black hat and put her silly fat head on the pavement, place it in position like a football, and then kick at it with Selina's boots until her own brain-box isn't quite what it was.

'I must go. The shops —'

'Doing the shopping for Nannie, are you, dear?'

'Goodbye.'

'I'll drop in over the weekend, shall I, see how Nannie is?'

'No. No, it's — I think she wants to be —'

'Don't you fret youself, dear, I'm not going to be tact-less. But I've felt bad, not keeping properly in touch when your Nan and I were once such bosom pals.' She bounces emphatically so that her own bosoms nod in agreement.

I don't know what to do. She can't go round there, not this weekend, not when Nan and Auntie Win will be in such a state over me. I see them sitting in the kitchen, Auntie Win screaming, Nan scraping. I feel as if Nan's potato knife is scraping at the inside of my stomach. I don't want to think about them, I'm not going to feel sorry yet. It's their fault, it's her fault, Mrs Roberts, why did she have to start?

'They're all right, really, Mrs Roberts. I wouldn't bother going round if I were you.'

She stares at me, settling her hat even further down her head so that her eyebrows disappear.

'I think I'm the best judge, dear,' she says sharply, trying to put me in my place.

But I can't be kept there any more. I'm kick kick kicking her with Selina's boots, and now I kick up in the air and soar right over her, and as I soar I shout 'They don't *want* you to come round. Why don't you just leave them alone and mind your own business?'

I shout it. Oh God, I've really said it. The words hiss through her hat and take effect. I start running before she can reply. She calls after me indignantly but I don't take any notice.

I've done it. I've really done it.

Only what's the point? It won't keep her away. She'll go straight round to Nan's and complain about me to Auntie Win. They'll feel even worse. And what will they do? Will Auntie Win come round to Selina's to drag me back home in disgrace? There's no point waiting. I might just as well go home now. Well, I've got to buy some food first. And then I might as well have a meal. I so badly want to have one special meal with Selina.

Some of the shops are shutting already but the little delicatessen is open. I wander round the shelves with a wire basket and my hand in the woolly glove is Selina's hand, calm and confident. It chooses with care. Asparagus soup. A bag of Hovis rolls in the shape of little loaves. Normandy butter. Sparkling grape juice. A mushroom quiche. Little salads in cartons, tomato and sweetcorn and runner beans. A special frozen raspberry mousse. And little chocolate dragees in a gold box.

109

I get frightened when the man behind the counter adds it all up and tells me the total, but Selina's purse is fat with five pound notes and I know it won't worry her. I'm not going to let it worry me either. All right, I will go home later, but I'm not going to think about Nan and Auntie Win now. I will switch them off, as if they are stuck inside a television set. I picture them flickering on a screen. My hand reaches out, huge and all powerful, and I twiddle a knob. Nan and Auntie Win are startled into statues, and then the screen goes blank and all that remains of them is a tiny little white light right in the centre.

The light stays with me, it's there behind my eyelids even when I close my eyes, but if I keep blinking maybe it will go away. I pay for the food and carry it out carefully in a big brown paper sack. I feel each item through the stout paper, going over the whole menu in my head, my mouth starting to water. The light is still there but it's only a pinprick after all so what do I care.

It's really dark now and it's further back to Selina's than I thought. When I get to her house at last the lights all seem to be out, although there's an odd flickering glow behind her bedroom curtains. I don't need to knock at the door, I've got her key in her handbag. I struggle inside with the sack of food and stand still in the hall.

'Selina?'

Perhaps she's gone back to sleep. I take the food into the kitchen and then go upstairs.

'Selina,' I say again, outside her bedroom door.

It's closed. I don't think she can be asleep. There's that flickering line of light underneath her door. I don't know what it is. I don't know what she's doing. I fumble with the door handle. My hands are shaking.

Selina is kneeling on the floor inside a silver pentacle, wearing a long white robe. She's arranged her amber beads in her newly-washed hair. It's still slightly damp, sliding down past her waist, hiding her hands. A small silver bowl of clear liquid shines at her knees. Candles

110

flicker at every point of the pentacle, and their light gives Selina's face a strange golden glow.

I tiptoe closer, as if I'm at a shrine. She looks at me, her eyes glittering, and then she throws her hair back over her shoulders with two quick shrugs. She's holding a little black velvet bag in one hand and a knife in the other, a *knife*. She's clasping the black handle, pointing the thin gleaming blade straight at me.

I gasp and Selina giggles.

'Don't be silly, sister. There's no need to be afraid. You are an initiate of the silver pentacle. Cast off your outer garments and come and join me.'

'Selina, I —'

'Come,' she says sharply.

I take off her boots and scarf and gloves. I take off my coat. I'm about to step inside the pentacle but Selina shakes her head.

'I've prepared a robe for you,' she says, nodding towards her bed, where a clean nightdress is neatly folded.

I don't dare argue with her. I undo my green winter frock and pull it over my head, horribly aware of Selina's glittering eyes. I wonder if I'm supposed to take off all my clothes so that I'm naked under the nightdress. I pull it on hurriedly over my petticoat, determined not to go that far.

'Join me, sister.'

I step inside the silver star shape. It's not a makeshift tinsel affair this time, it's a silvery steel shape with a raised edge, like a giant biscuit cutter. There is room for me to kneel comfortably before Selina. She nods approvingly as I copy her position. Then she aims the knife. I'm not going to scream, although I can't stop myself shaking. I have to trust her. She raises the blade to my forehead. She touches my skin with its ice-cold point.

'Welcome to the Sabbat of Selina, symbolic child of the great Moon Goddess, whom we worship within the silver pentacle.'

111

She moves the knife downwards, touches my left breast, my right breast, my left knee, my right knee.

'You now bear the indelible magic mark of the silver pentacle. Kiss the blade of the sacred weapon.'

I kiss the tip of the knife and Selina kisses it too, and then lightly scores the palm of her left hand. There's a tiny spurt of scarlet blood.

'Hold out your own hand,' she commands.

She takes hold of it because it is trembling so much. She makes a little stab with the knife and I stare at my own blood. Selina clasps my left palm, mingling our blood.

'We are now true sisters of the silver pentacle,' she says, and she leans forward and kisses me on either cheek. She is burning hot and I can see the swollen glands swelling her white neck.

'Look into my eyes, sister. We are both vessels for the power of the light and the power of the shade. Shall we choose the pale power of the Great Goddess's waxing silver light? Shall we choose the dark power of her waning shadows?'

I can see little flickering candle flames reflected in her great dark eyes. Our palms are still clasped, slightly sticky with blood. A pulse throbs in my hand and I don't know whether it's mine or Selina's. It's as if we are truly joined, sisters since the womb, sisters within it, sisters of dark eternity. And I want to choose the dark. I want the power of the dark waning shadows. I want the darkest power of all, the blackest shade. I want it and yet when I stare into her dark eyes and see it there I'm scared.

'Let's choose the power of light this time.'

Selina's eyes flicker scornfully.

'Boring!' she hisses, but then she composes herself, lets go my hand, and lifts the candlestick at the top point of the pentacle.

'Hail to thee, great shining Goddess of the sky. Send down your silvery light to gladden our hearts as we glorify your name. We wish to magnify your moonliness, evoking the power of your waxing silver light. Send down the beams of your brightness to us tonight, great sister of the sky. Let the power pulse in our bodies and flower in our souls,' Selina cries. The flames flicker and the blue smoke spirals upwards. She turns to me. 'Get up, May. Praise our great Goddess. Feel her holy power.'

I get up and Selina holds the candlestick up high, her arms taut with the effort.

'Praise the mighty Moon Goddess,' says Selina, flinging her head right back.

I fling my head back too, and see a great silvery moon there in Selina's bedroom. After a second of true lunacy I see that it's simply silver paper cut out and stuck on the ceiling. I stare hard at the shining orb, the blood beating in my throat, and I feel as if some strange power is stealing into my soul. I stare upwards and chant praises until the moon blurs and the room starts swirling round me.

'Sit,' gasps Selina, and somehow she steadies the wavering candlestick. She puts it back in place at the point of the pentacle. Little beads of sweat shine on her forehead like miniature moons. She breathes deeply, smiling triumphantly.

'There. We have the power while we remain within the pentacle. We can ask a question and make one wish. The question first?'

I nod and she picks up the little black velvet bag. She unties the ribbon at its neck and carefully tips three small smooth stones onto the carpet. One is a slither of real moonstone, milky pale. Selina picks it up reverently.

'This is the moonstone, the stone of the Great Goddess herself, the most magical of all.' She picks up the bright blue stone. 'This is lapis lazuli, the stone of Jupiter, the god of good fortune.' She picks up the last stone, a little egg of glossy black. 'And this is the all powerful onyx of Saturn.'

She cups her hands and shakes the stones, making them rattle.

'Ask a question, sister, and I will cast the stones. If the moonstone lands nearest the lapis then the answer will be yes. If it lands nearest the onyx then the answer will be no.'

I swallow as she shakes the stones.

'Do I have to ask the question out loud?'

'Of course,' says Selina, smiling.

I daren't trust her. I can't ask it. So what shall I ask?

I look her straight in the eyes.

'Is Selina really my friend?'

She raises her eyebrows but her smile doesn't waver. She shakes the stones one more time and then lets them fall. The moonstone is exactly midway between the lapis and the onyx. We both stare at them and then burst out laughing.

'My go now,' says Selina, scooping up the stones. 'Right. Will I make a conquest of a certain man I know?'

'That's cheating! You've got to say who,' I say indignantly, wishing I'd been that artful.

Selina knows full well that she makes the rules. She throws the stones. The moonstone lands so close to the lapis that they almost touch.

'Ah!' she says.

'Can I ask another question?'

'Sorry. But never mind, you've still got a wish,' says Selina, dropping the stones back into their velvet bag. She carefully moves the silver bowl, its liquid rippling, and places it in front of me.

'Gaze into the molten moonlight, sister,' she says softly. 'Stare into the liquid light. Look for your heart's desire. Scan the surface and see it there and then use the divine powers of our Great Goddess. Wish with all your might and use the silver second sight.'

I stare at the silver water. I stare and stare at the sparkling surface. I see my own face dimly reflected. I stare until it wavers. It dissolves into a pale moon. A white sphere that stretches into another face. I start to see features. Two dark eyes shaded with glass. A boyish

114

nose, a wry smile, a short spikey haircut. It's as if I'm painting the face on the surface of the water.

'You are my heart's desire,' I whisper. 'I want you.'

# Chapter 15

'Of course, there's one way to cinch things with old Rob,' says Selina, delicately licking her spoonful of raspberry mousse. She sounds so innocent but she can't stop her eyes glittering. Well, she can't catch me, even if I'm so woozy with wine that the silver paper moon on the ceiling is spinning round and round on a little orbit of my own invention.

'Rob?' I say, oh so casually. Not too obvious though. None of the Rob-who? 'You mean Robin Campbell?'

Selina laughs in acknowledgement of my performance.

'All right, May. But you can't fool me. He is your heart's desire, isn't he?'

'No! Oh I–I think he's quite attractive. I like him, but he's much too old. I don't go for men that age.'

I sound so plausible that her conviction wavers. She pours herself a cup of coffee from the jug and unwraps a chocolate mint. She bites it neatly in half with her sharp white teeth.

'I've seen the way you look at him. You go bright red whenever he so much as blinks.'

'I go bright red all the time. Look, I'm blushing now,' I say, feeling my cheeks. 'Or is that the wine?'

'Have some more, go on. Let's finish the bottle.'

'No. I've had enough as it is. Too much.'

'Well, it's better than that dreary old grape juice, eh?'

'Don't be so ungrateful.'

'It was my money, for God's sake. But the rest was okay, I suppose.'

'It was a wonderful imaginative meal — and you've eaten it all up, every scrap. You must be getting better.'

'Maybe. Although I still feel pretty peculiar.'

'That's because you're drunk too.'

'I do not get drunk on a glass or two of wine, my child,' says Selina grandly. 'You're still blushing, did you know?'

'It must be the wine. Or I'm getting your bug.'

'Oh well. We can keep each other company. I might even let you share my sick bed if you're very good. You are staying over, aren't you?'

'I'm not sure I dare. I'll be in enough trouble as it is.' I take another gulp of wine to wash the worry away.

'You've got to stay. I'm ill, I can't be left on my own,' says Selina, rubbing her neck. 'I wish it would stop hurting so much.'

'You should have wished to get better when we were in the pentacle.'

'I'll have a little word with the Great Goddess now.' She looks up at the ceiling, holding her wine glass aloft. 'Circle my neck with your silvery powers and ease my agony, okay?' She spills some of her wine and it dribbles up her arm. She swears and licks at it like a cat. She's just as drunk as I am, no matter what she says.

'Watch out. The Great Goddess might take you literally. If you go on burbling about circling your neck and putting you out of your agony she might reach right down from the sky and strangle you.'

'Do not mock the powers of the great Moon Goddess,' says Selina. 'Ugh, I'm all sticky, I'll have to have another bath. And let's have some more wine, mm? Run and fetch another bottle, little May. Red this time, we don't want to mess about waiting while it chills.'

'We can't! What will your father say?'

'It's my house. My wine. My friend.'

'Best friend? And sister witch?'

'Indis-disput-ably,' says Selina, lifting the bottle for the dregs. 'More wine, chop chop. And then I'll tell you how to cinch things with your Heart's Desire. The mysterious anonymous male who *isn't* Rob Campbell. At least I presume it's a bloke? Or is it creeping out of the closet time, mm?'

'Don't be daft. And why should my Heart's Desire be anyone? Why couldn't I have wished for a new coat or boots or —'

'I saw your face. You don't get that worked up over *clothes*.'

She's right, although she doesn't understand how much it would mean to me to have her sort of clothes. As I walk unsteadily downstairs to fetch another bottle of wine her nightdress floats lightly round my body — her *old* nightdress — white lawn with white smocking across the chest and lace at the neck and sleeves and all round the billowing hem. It makes me feel like a bride. I start humming the Wedding March in time to my steps: Da dum da dum Da dum da dum Da dum da *da* dum da Da dum da dum. I clasp the new bottle of wine as if it is my bridal bouquet and as I stagger up the stairs Robin is with me, his arm through mine, mine, my Heart's Desire.

Selina expertly uncorks the bottle and pours me a full glass. Our hands are unsteady and a little claret splashes onto my lap.

'How very symbolic,' says Selina, looking at the red stains.

'What is this new charm?'

'It isn't exactly a charm — more a ceremony. An old custom. It's supposed to be when the moon is full. I don't know whether it is or not but never mind about that, *our* moon couldn't be fuller and fatter,' she says, looking up at the silver paper and tracing its shape in the air with her finger. 'Is it going round and round?' she asks, giggling.

'Yes, it *is*.'

'Or is it us?' says Selina, swaying and circling. She spills more wine, on her own robe this time. 'Oh God. And it doesn't wash off, does it? This is my mother's proper Priestess robe, she'll go crackers.' She drinks

118

more wine determinedly. 'She *is* crackers. So it won't make any difference. And she can't boss me about any more, not now I'm practically grown up. I'm only in thrall to the Great Goddess, isn't that right, Silver Highness of the sky?' She looks up at the paper moon again and I see her eyes revolving. 'Round and round,' she murmurs. 'Round and round and round.' She sounds as if she's almost in a trance but then she looks at me. 'That's what you've got to do. Go round and round.'

'What, round and round in the pentacle?' I say, picking up my skirts and stepping inside.

'Oh no. It has to be outdoors. In the moonlight. You have to run around a sacred grove. Well, we haven't got one of them, but there's a willow tree in the front garden, I'm sure that will do splendidly. Get inside the branches so that you're in its secret  enclosure and run round seven times, widdershins.'

'With my *shins?*'

'Are you taking the piss?' she says sharply.

'No. But I think you are.'

'I am pissed. I know that,' says Selina, snorting with laughter. 'Oh God, feel my *head.* I should be in bed. I shall go to bed — in a minute. Let's get you sorted out, little sister. *Widdershins.* Anticlockwise. Against the path of the sun. In the sly silvery steps of the Moon Goddess, got it? That way round.' She gesticulates. 'Okay?'

'Okay. I suppose. And that's all I have to do? Run round this willow seven times —'

'Without being seen. Which will be easy, because you'll be inside the branches — and anyway it's pitch black out there. And if you succeed the charm will work.'

'You have that on the absolute utmost authority I take it?'

'I warned you, don't take the piss, May. This isn't a joke, you know. You can't mess around with the power of the shade.' She comes closer, standing over me, her face stern. 'You can't back out now. You're committed. If you invoke the power of the Moon Goddess you have to use it — or it will use you. She will consume you.'

'You've been fooling about too,' I say nervously.

'I know what I'm doing. I've been a full initiate since the age of thirteen. I've taken part in the most secret of the ceremonies. The silver pentacle has five points. You have only celebrated the power of the first point. You don't know what you're meddling with, May. Think about the power of the moon. All the tides of the world are controlled by its magnetic pull. All the women in the world bleed in a bodily metaphor, to show we are all handmaidens of the Great Mother Goddess. She shines within you, sister. We have spilled blood in our obeisance. Mock her powers and she will spill more blood. Glorify her name and she will grant you your Heart's Desire.

'All right, all right. I'll do it. But do I have to do it now? I don't want to go out in the dark.'

'The moon doesn't usually shine in the middle of the morning,' Selina says irritably.

'It's going to be cold out there. Can I borrow your coat? It's much warmer than my old duffel.'

'You can wear it until you get to the willow, I suppose. But then you'll have to put up with the cold. You've got to be naked while you're actually working the charm.'

'Naked?'

'Of course.'

'No I don't. You're just saying that to tease,' I argue feebly. 'I think you're making this whole thing up as you go along.'

'Am I?' says Selina, her head on one side. 'Am I? Look, I'm doing all this for your benefit, you ungrateful little squirt. You kept pestering me to tell you more about witchcraft, didn't you? And now you've asked me how to get your Heart's Desire.'

'I've wished for it already.'

'Yes, but this is the really powerful wish, the one that will make it come completely true.'

'So long as I run round your front garden stark

naked? Selina! I shall get arrested.'

'No-one will see you. That's the point. Wear my coat into the garden. Drop it when you get to the willow. Get inside those long branches. It's just like a cave. I used to hide inside it when I was little and no-one could ever find me. Do your running. You'll keep warm that way, won't you? And then — then you'll have your Heart's Desire. I think that's a very fair bargain. It'll only take you two minutes, for God's sake. Two measly minutes in exchange for your Heart's Desire.'

'So why don't you do it too?'

'There's no necessity. The men I want don't seem to need supernatural encouragement.'

'There's no need to be so bloody smug about it,' I say, starting to lose my temper. She thinks I'm too shy and scared to streak round her garden. She's all set to scoff at me. Well, I'll show her.

'Okay,' I say, and I take off her nightdress. I take off my bra and tights and knickers too, boldly, as if I don't give a damn. I stick my bare feet back into Selina's boots and shrug her coat round my shoulders. It's a big black and white tweed that is large even on Selina. It swamps me, sweeping right down to the ground like a great cloak. It seems an appropriate garment.

'I won't be long,' I say nonchalantly. 'Don't you dare look out your window. I don't want you mucking up the charm.'

I sweep out, although the boots and the wine make me stagger sideways. I hear Selina cackling with laughter but it sounds a little forced. I'll show her. I'll do the silly charm properly. I will achieve my Heart's Desire. Do you know that, Robin Campbell? Are you thinking of me? You will be in a minute. You won't be able to get me out of your head. I'm going to be in there all the time, driving you crazy.

The heavy tweed coat feels so odd against my bare skin. I feel as if I'm being embraced by a huge beast. I open the front door. The cold hits me. I stare out into the dark, holding on to the door for support. I hear

121

someone walking along the pavement. They are on the other side of a tall hedge, and anyway I'm clothed from top to bottom in thick tweed, but I still hide behind the door until the footsteps die away. I wait, my heart thudding. My cheeks are burning although I'm shivering underneath the coat. Perhaps I really am getting Selina's bug. I must be feverish taking part in this silly prank. Or drunk. Or just plain daft.

Well, I know I'm both, but who cares, I'm going to do it. I step away from the door, leaving it on the latch. I don't want to get locked out. That would be a fine trick for Selina to play on me. I peer up at her window. I think I saw the curtains move, but it's hard to be sure. And then the dark lightens eerily and I look up past the house at the moon. The large and luminous silver globe is so beautiful that it sucks all the breath out of me. I can see why she is worshipped. The old man-in-the-moon rhymes Grandad chanted were so silly. The moon could never be a man and that silver light could never shine from anything as banal as blue cheese. I know it's really made of volcanic rock and an American man took a gigantic step on it but now I'm ready to cast off my coat and indulge in pagan practices, I am ready to worship the moon as a white goddess, the silver orb of the sky. An orb. It is round. A perfect circle amongst the stars. It is a full moon.

I can't back out now. I glide across the garden, part of the magic, part of the moonlight. I find the willow easily enough but I circle the outside of it in despair. The branches have lost most of their leaves. The fronds hang forlornly, wispy and inadequate. They won't hide me properly. I can hear Selina's mocking laugh inside my head. But I'm not going to listen. I'm going to show her. I'm going to achieve my Heart's Desire. It is a full moon and I'm not going to waste its magic.

I push aside the willow fronds and stand right in the centre, touching the trunk. The branches still offer some kind of covering. It is very dark. And who can see me anyway? Selina would have to hang right out of her window to catch a glimpse of me.

I undo the buttons of the tweed coat and fling it dramatically to the ground. The cold air on my body is startling, so extreme that it's almost exhilarating. It's much more worrying taking off Selina's boots. I'm terrified I'll step on a slug or a spider. I start running, wanting to get it over as quickly as possible. I'm not sure about the widdershins part and I have to pause and then start whirling round the other way to get it right. Once. Twice. Three times. I'm getting so dizzy already. And there's a root sticking up sideways, I keep tripping on it, I'm scared I'll go headlong. Four times. Or is it five? Where did I start? Oh God, the whole tree has started spinning with me. I'd better keep on going. Say six times now. Just one more. Although it might be safer to do another circle in case I've miscounted. If only everything would stop whirling. I feel so sick. I'm going to be sick. But I can't stop, I can't break the spell now, I have to have my Heart's Desire ... What's that? Footsteps. It's just someone — no, two people — on the pavement on the other side of the hedge. They can't see me. And they'll be gone in a minute. The footsteps have stopped. I stop too, because I've done it, I've gone round the willow seven times widdershins, naked in the light of the full moon. I lean against the trunk, gasping for breath, too sick and dizzy to search for my coat. The footsteps are still stopped but the voices are there.

'It's a bit posh, isn't it?'

'Well, she's got class, hasn't she?'

'So don't you think we're maybe wasting our time?'

'No! She was giving us the real come-on, I'm telling you.'

'Giving you. So you go and knock on her door and chat her up. And I'll push off home.'

'Don't be so daft. You come too. She *liked* you. And anyway, there's that friend. She wasn't that bad.'

'So you have the friend.'

'Look, we'll play it by ear, okay? Let's go and knock her up then.'

'Knock her up! Better watch out you don't.'

'I just want to have the chance, mate. So come on.'

They're coming in the gate! I feel frantically for Selina's coat. I can't find it, oh God, where is it? They go up the garden path. I clasp the trunk of the willow as they pass, pressing myself flat, closing my eyes. They're so near. They could reach under the fronds and touch me. But they walk straight past, on up the path, to the front door.

It is still on the latch. I can't hear them properly now. They hesitate, arguing, for several minutes. Then one knocks on the door and they step inside. And I am stuck out here in the garden, stark naked.

# Chapter 16

I stand clutching the tree, stupidly staring at the front door as if I believed I could spirit myself inside it, fully clothed. I've got to find the coat. That's the first thing. It can't have vanished. Which side did I put it? And oh God, what's that, what have I got hold of, smooth and slippery, it's a snake, a *snake* ... I fling it wildly to the far end of the garden. A snake wouldn't land with a thud. And then I find another one and it isn't a pair of snakes, it's a pair of boots, Selina's boots, and I'm never going to find the other one, not now when the garden is mapped with shadows in the moonlight. I put the remaining boot on my foot and hobble round the tree, searching for the coat. I trip on the root and this time I go flying, landing on my hands and knees. Tears well in my eyes. It's so cold I'm scared the drops will freeze and dangle from my lashes. I straighten up painfully and go on searching, and at last I find the coat at the very edge of the fronds. I flap it frantically, thinking of all the spiders and slugs that might have crept into its folds, and then wrap it round me. I do up all the buttons and then stand free of the tree, panting after all the panic, trying to think what to do.

I can't face Selina and those two hateful boys, not clad solely in a coat three sizes too big for me and one muddy boot. So shall I go home? But how can I arrive looking like this? Nan and Auntie Win will think I've been raped. They'll call the police. Perhaps they've called the police anyway. I've *got* to go home. I can't stay away all weekend. And yet how can I go home without my own clothes?

I hear more footsteps along the pavement and I rush instinctively towards the house, although the footsteps carry on past the gate and along the other side of the hedge. And then I see a gleam of light around the edge of the front door. At least they didn't shut it, they left it on the latch. Perhaps I can creep in and up the stairs to Selina's bedroom without them seeing me. Unless they're *in* Selina's bedroom. I know what she's like. Only she doesn't give a damn about these boys. They're the ones who tried to chat her up in W.H. Smiths. She won't want anything to do with them. Yet they're still in the house with her. Perhaps *they* crept up the stairs. Perhaps they've got hold of her now. Perhaps they're raping her — and I'm standing out here, dithering.

I hobble up to the house in my one boot, wincing as I cross the gravel. When I'm on the doorstep I wriggle out of the boot and then tiptoe inside in my bare feet. The light is on in the hall and I stare down at myself in horror. My feet are filthy and when I hold up the hem of the coat I see the mud is halfway up my legs.

I hear Selina laughing. She's downstairs in the living room. I can hear them too, they're laughing — perhaps they're all having a good laugh at me. I run up the stairs and into Selina's bedroom. She's blown the candles out and hidden the silver pentacle. It is just an ordinary girl's bedroom, apart from the scrap of silver paper stuck to the ceiling.

They're laughing so much I can still hear them even up here. I want to get into my own clothes so badly I'm not even going to bother to wash. My legs won't show under my woollen tights. I pull my frock over my head and then sit at Selina's dressing table, brushing my tangled hair back from my face. I remember Selina's strange expression as she invoked the power of the moon goddess. Is there a silvery gleam in my own face? I stare into the mirror and I see right through my own eyes, I'm looking right to my Heart's Desire. Rob is

126

there, looking back at me, smiling because I am his, and he is mine. I've wished it in the water of the silver chalice and I've evoked the widdershins charm in the light of the full moon. I've done it so what do I care about those stupid boys downstairs and Selina?

I stand up and put on my own old duffle coat. It's no use. I do care. I diminish into a white mouse. I scurry downstairs. Not quietly enough.

'Who's that?' Selina calls. 'May? Is that you?'

For all she knows I could still be stark naked. I suppose that's the idea.

'I'm going now,' I say.

'What do you mean, you're going? Come here. May, come *here*.'

I walk into the living room as commanded. She looks at me, obviously disappointed I'm just my ordinary shabby self. The boys look disappointed too. They are the W.H. Smith pair. They're dressed up for Saturday night so they look marginally better. The darker cockier one is all sub-Scot Crolla in his flash waistcoat and trendy jacket. The small sandy one is in a leather coat that looks as if it belongs to his big brother. He creaks whenever he moves. He's fidgetting because he's stuck in a chair while his friend is sitting on the sofa right beside Selina.

They are obviously stunned by her. She looks incredible in her long white robe in the middle of the ice white room. Her cheeks are pink with fever and her eyes look darker than ever.

'May, meet Ben and Pete.'

'Hi, May,' says Ben, the dark one. 'Where did you spring from?'

'May's been looking after me,' Selina says sweetly.

'Yes, well, I'm off now.'

'I thought you were staying for the weekend?' says Selina. 'Don't let Ben and Pete frighten you away. They're quite harmless, aren't you, boys?'

I could kill her. I blush as they all grin at me.

'No, I've got to go.'

'Look, my mate was hoping you'd be here,' Ben says quickly. 'Don't go, May. You want her to stay, don't you, Pete?'

Sandy Pete looks sullen, as well he might. He doesn't want me to stay at all. And I don't want to stay for him. I can't stand him. I can't stand Ben either. I'm *glad* they don't fancy me. As if I would ever want to get involved with two stupid schoolboys when I've got Rob.

I'm not going to say another word. I walk right out of the white room and down the hall. Selina catches me at the front door.

'What are you playing at?' she demands.

'Nothing. I'm going home. That's all.'

'But you promised you'd stay!'

'I can't. Not now.'

'So you're going off in a huff just because of those two idiots in there?'

'Well, they *are* idiots. So why are you wasting your time with them?'

'I didn't let them in. You did. A fine trick to play on me — leaving me lying on my sickbed and inviting those two sex-mad schoolkids up the stairs.'

'I did not. They went in by themselves. I left the door on the latch.'

'Why didn't you stop them?'

'I was hiding by the willow — as you well know. I wasn't going to leap out at them stark naked and tell them it wasn't a good time to come visiting,' I hiss at her.

Selina giggles and I risk taking hold of her hand.

'Selina. Can't you get rid of them? We were having such a great time together,' I whisper. 'I did the charm. Seven times widdershins.'

'Shut up! They're probably eavesdropping.'

'Couldn't you tell them to go and then we could do some more — you know ...'

Selina snatches her hand away.

'Really May. You sound positively perverted,' she says, wiping her hand on her gown as if it were contaminated.

128

I feel as if I'm on fire. My eyes burn too and Selina sees the tears.

'Oh for God's sake. It was a joke. Why are you always so soft?'

'Why are you always so hard?'

Selina smiles as if I've paid her a compliment.

'Like a diamond, the hardest stone in the world? A shining silvery moon diamond?' she says tantalisingly.

'Here, Selina! What are you up to?' Ben calls, coming into the hall. 'Trying to persuade little May to stay?' He comes up to me and actually puts his arm round my shoulder. 'You stay with us, sweetheart, you'll have a great time.'

Selina splutters with laughter but he doesn't seem to mind.

'Leave her alone, Ben. Go back in the other room, go on. Look, are you listening to me? Piss off, there's a good boy.'

He doesn't even seem to mind that. He trots off and Selina sighs.

'What a creep,' she says softly.

'So why put up with him? And that awful Pete. You've got heaps better boyfriends than them. What about Bruno?'

'Bruno is otherwise engaged at the moment,' Selina says sourly.

'We were otherwise engaged too.'

'Okay okay. But I thought we could have a bit of fun with those two wallies.' Selina smiles at me beguilingly. 'Go on, stick around, May. It's about time you got to know some boys anyway. You're positively retarded in that respect.'

'Selina! Come *on*. I want you.' Whispers and then great guffaws.

'I'd sooner stay retarded,' I say, and I open the front door.

'So you're going to push off and leave me?' Selina asks. 'Oh, that's really great.' She touches her forehead. 'Me with a high temperature and glands bulging right out of my neck.'

'Selina, Selina!' They're both shouting now. 'Come *on*, sweetheart.'

'They sound as if they've got glands bulging right out of their trousers,' I say in disgust.

'Yes, well, it's me they want, not you.'

'I know that.'

'And no wonder. Look at you. You look about six in that stupid old duffle coat. And you're hopeless with boys, you just blush and bumble about, you haven't a clue.'

I'm out of the front door and down the path but her clear voice carries across the garden. I can still seem to hear it when I'm right at the other end of the road. I don't know why I'm crying. It isn't as if she's said anything I don't know. And I don't care anyway. I don't. I've got Rob. My Heart's Desire. But have I? Selina called something else. I put my hands over my ears but I couldn't help hearing.

'You looked such an idiot capering round and round that old tree. I could see you all the time. I nearly wet myself laughing.'

She was just being spiteful because I'm going home. She couldn't really have seen me, not from her bedroom window. Though she could easily have gone to another window. She probably would look, to laugh at me. And if she saw me then the charm is useless. Although I don't really believe in magic, do I? I know Selina's mostly making it up. It's just a silly game she plays to get power over me. That bit works. But I don't seem to have power over anyone. Rob is my Heart's Desire but why should I be the desire of *his* heart? He was just feeling sorry for me because I'm such an odd one out at school. And I write silly stories for him. But that's all they are. Fairy stories. Babyish little fairy stories. I'm too old for all this Fairies and Witches nonsense. There's no such thing as magic.

I stand still in the street. I look up at the moon, wiping my eyes.

130

'It's all rubbish,' I say out loud. 'I don't believe in any of it. The power of the light and the power of the shade. It's all silly superstition. There's no such thing as a moon goddess.'

My hand smarts where Selina cut it. It feels wet. It shines darkly in the moonlight.

The cut has only opened up because I've been clenching my fist. Of course it isn't an omen. The moon goddess hasn't got any power. And I haven't any power either, that's perfectly obvious.

What about Grandad?

It wasn't my fault. It was nothing to do with me. He was ill, he'd had angina for years. Worrying about me. No, that's not true, he said I was no trouble, he never told me off like Nan and Auntie Win, he played funny games with me and sat me on his lap and made me feel that he loved me almost as much as Amy. It's so unfair that he had to die and I'm left with Nan and Auntie Win and — What are they going to say to me?

I remember the things I said to them and I start to feel sick. What am I going to do? It isn't really that late now. I was much later than this the day I went out with Selina and Bruno and Mick.

It's all Selina's fault. I'm mad to want her for a friend. She's always so hateful to me. She doesn't care about me, she just likes to lead me on and then laugh at me. Of course she was watching when I ran round the willow tree. I hate her. I really hate her. I'm not going to let her have power over me any more.

If she hadn't phoned today then none of this would have happened. I'd be sitting safely at home with Nan and Auntie Win. I've got to go home now. I've got to face them. I think I'm going to be sick. I suppose I'm still drunk. They'll be able to smell the drink on me. They don't drink at all at home, only Harvey's Bristol Cream at Christmas, and there's the little bottle of brandy for medicinal purposes. I think of Nan trying to get poor dead Grandad to swig from the bottle and I start crying again.

There aren't any lights on when I get home. I run into the kitchen, expecting Nan and Auntie Win to be sprawling on the lino, felled by my fury — but the kitchen is empty. I try the living room, I even peep in the dining room, but there's no-one there.

I'm halfway up the stairs when Auntie Win comes out of the bathroom. She's in her quilted dressing gown, her hair in rollers. She looks as if her face is tightly pinned too.

'Oh Auntie Win, I'm sorry, I'm so sorry.'

She doesn't even blink. She pads along to her bedroom without a glance in my direction. I run after her and grab hold of her slippery dressing gown.

'Auntie Win, please. I'm *sorry*. I promise I won't ever go off like that again. I didn't mean what I said. Please talk to me. I can't stand it when you won't talk to me.'

I don't exist. Auntie Win tweaks her quilting from my hand and shuts her bedroom door in my face. I'm left by myself on the dark landing. I switch on the light defiantly and run to Nan and Grandad's room. I open the door and creep inside.

'Nan. Nan, it's me, May. Nan, please wake up.'

Nan snores softly, looking horribly lost at the edge of the big double bed. I wonder if I dare clamber in beside her. I approach her hesitantly. I can see her face clearly from the light on the landing. She looks so *old*. I stare at the puckers in her skin, the sag of her mouth. If it wasn't for the purr of her breath I'd think she was dead. I don't dare sleep with her. What if I woke in the morning and found her stiffened beside me?

'I'm sorry, Nan,' I whisper and creep back to my own room.

Amy's room. She's there, smiling. I slam her down on her face and get my notebook and pen.

Two great black crows had lost their only chick and were mourning their empty nest when they spied a little peasant girl

132

wandering in the forest. She stopped beneath their tree, pausing to etch a heart on the old bark. She was a very tiny child, dressed in dark worsted. The crows were very large, with sharp talons. They looked at the child with eager eyes, they looked at each other, and then they swooped down to the foot of the tree. Two talons fastened on each frail shoulder, and then the child was lifted screaming into thin air. They dropped her right into their reeking nest and sat on her to stop her squawking. They had a new chick now.

She wasn't a patch on the old. She struggled and spat and wouldn't eat up all her juicy pink worms. Her dark covering fell off, exposing useless white flesh, and her long red feathers were no use at all when it came to flying.

The crows pecked her to punish her. They pecked at her arms, at her legs, at her thin white neck. They even pecked at her forehead, horribly near her eyes. Her only respite was at night, when the two crows slept. The child squeezed herself out from under their wings and looked up at the silver moon. A nightingale started singing. It sang of the dark woods, the rippling water, the soft clouds and the silver jewel in the sky. It sang of love and death, happiness and heartbreak, while the child listened and wept. She wished she had the courage to clamber out of the nest and climb right down to the ground. It was such a long way down. She could so easily fall. And the crows might wake and catch her and peck out her eyes as a punishment.

So she stayed crouched in the nest. The ageing crows pecked at the cowering child

133

until the nest was slimey with blood. The twigs started rotting until one day the whole nest suddenly fell apart. The crows cawed and flapped their wings in fury. The child screamed as she tumbled downwards. She crashed in and out of the branches and landed flat on her back amongst the brambles.

She was free at last but she could not move. Her body seemed broken. She lay there all the day long. Whenever she saw a bird in the sky she closed her eyes in case the crows were coming back. It grew dark and the silver moon shone in the sky and the nightingale sang — and far below in the brambles the child cried.

# Chapter 17

He stands at the front of the classroom in his black sweater, the red knitted heart a little lop-sided on his chest. He isn't very good at washing it. He's hung it up on a line, I can see faint peg marks pinching the shoulders, and it's stretched. It makes him look like a little boy lost inside his big sweater. I can't believe he's old enough to be my father. He looks so earnest and anxious standing in front of us, talking about seventeenth century Salem, trying to get us to see what it was really like. I wish I hadn't missed the lesson last week. They read Act One and Selina was Abigail.

I flick through my copy of *The Crucible,* trying to pick up the story. I know it's about witchcraft. I thought it would be weird old women, like the witches in *Macbeth.* But these are young girls — and oh my God, they've been conjuring spirits, drinking charms and dancing naked in the woods.

The class starts reading Act Two. Rob reads the part of John Procter himself, and big Maggie is his wife Elizabeth. I'm still hovering in Act One. Abigail used to work for the Procters. Abigail wanted John Procter and he fell helplessly in love with her. He picked Selina to be Abigail. He picked Selina.

I sit like a stone while they gabble through Act Two. It doesn't really work. Rob's good at acting and big Maggie's okay, but he picks Ruth for May Warren and she reads in a monotone even when she's meant to be weeping, and Judy isn't much better as Hale because she overacts, putting on this Ronald Regan voice that makes everyone giggle. Rob's starting to look worried. He looks up, straight at me, but I won't smile at him for reassurance. Let him sweat it out. He picked Selina for his Abigail.

Kath and Jen and Sarah and some of the others have stopped following the play. They're passing notes and whispering about some party at the weekend. Louise is openly turning the pages of *Just Seventeen*. Carol's combing her hair. There's still half the lesson left.

'Let's leave it there for now,' says Rob, shutting his book abruptly.

'Yeah, let's,' says Kath, laughing.

She's taken over Selina's role now she isn't here. She's really ill. I phoned her this morning on the way to school. I spoke to her mother, back from her weekend in Wales. Selina has got glandular fever. I asked if I could speak to her and her mother said she'd go and see, but when she came back she said Selina didn't feel up to it. Selina obviously isn't speaking to me because she thinks I deserted her on Saturday. She probably won't make friends with me for weeks. Her mother didn't sound a bit how I imagined. She was rather gushing and called me Sweetie. She didn't sound a bit like a witch.

Rob is talking about witchcraft now, hoping to grab back some of their attention. He's reading out extracts from some of the real witch trials, and the tortures and deaths are so startling that we are silenced.

'How could they *do* that?' says Kath, shivering.

'Do you think it could ever happen now?' Rob asks, relieved he's got us all with him again. All but one.

'How could it? You don't get witches nowadays.'

'Oh, I think you do. There's been a lot of recent interest in the Occult and Black Magic — and some feminists seriously seem to worship a pagan goddess,' says Rob.

I swallow while the others sneer.

'Just a load of nutters, that's all,' says Kath.

136

'Perhaps. But religious people still worry about witch-craft. Didn't you read about that church that was dese-crated by Black Magic followers? They had a bishop along to bless it again, didn't they.'

'Yes, but that's just a few extremists, isn't it?' Sarah argues seriously.

'Nutters, yes,' says Kath. 'Imagine believing in that sort of rubbish.'

'Don't you ever watch horror videos, Kath?' Rob asks.

'Yeah, sometimes.'

'Don't you find them scary?'

'No, they're just a laugh.'

'So you'd watch a really creepy video all by yourself at midnight, say, and not be the slightest bit scared? Come on, Kath,' says Rob, smiling at her.

My smile.

'Oh well. Of course I'd be scared — if I didn't have my boyfriend to cuddle up with,' says Kath daringly.

'But those horror videos aren't real, are they?' Sarah persists.

'Of course they're not real. I'm not saying that witch-craft is real. They weren't all convinced back in seven-teenth century Salem, were they? The girls were making it all up. But when everyone started believing them then the girls started believing it too.' He looks round, trying to convince us. He doesn't need to convince me. I wonder if he talked like this last week when Selina was here. Is that where she got it all from? Was it all a great hoax? I can hear the sound of her laughter now. Rob is smiling too. Perhaps she'll tell him.

'May?'

I start. Icicles, white peaks, frost ...

'What do you think?'

I'm not going to tell him what I think.

'I don't know,' I say, and I try to make it sound as if I don't care either.

And I don't care about him. His jumper looks stupid, stretched out of shape. And his silly hair. Why does he have it in those chic little spikes? He isn't *young*. He's a married man, his daughter's nearly my age. He's just a pathetic ageing trendy getting a kick out of chatting up young girls. Oh, he might be charming them now, jabbering away about astrology and horoscopes, making them see that they'll believe an entire twelfth of the world, billions of assorted Europeans and Africans and Asians are all going to meet an interesting stranger or receive good news in the post, so why is it so unlikely that a group of ignorant and uneducated adolescent girls would start believing in the power of potions and poppets — he's working his own little spell, they've stopped whispering and combing their hair, they've put away their magazines and they're laughing at his jokes, leaning forward to listen — but I am not enchanted. I stare stonily at that ridiculous red heart. He is not *my* Heart's Desire.

Who is? I haven't got anyone at all now. Boys are never going to start liking me. Look at those two at Selina's. And Selina isn't even speaking to me now. Neither is Auntie Win. She still hasn't said a word. Nan talks but she cries too, which is even worse. I think she might have started thinking that it's my fault Grandad isn't here any more. I wish he hadn't died. That's when it all started going wrong. No, it was when this stupid show-off first came into this classroom and made me start doodling a little black heart. But that was after stepping into the silver pentacle. That's when it really started. When I became a witch.

But it's not true. It's simple superstition, as Robin Campbell is demonstrating right this minute.

'So who started it?' asks Sarah.

'It was Abigail, wasn't it?' says Kath.

'So it was all her fault, was it?' says Sarah.

They discuss Abigail, how clever she is, and how dangerous, and it's as if they're all talking about Selina too. They even keep glancing at her empty desk.

'But Abigail doesn't really start the trouble, does she?' says Rob. 'Look at the play again, right at the beginning. She does her best to deny things, to hush it all up, doesn't she?'

'It was Tituba,' says Sarah.

'Oh great, it's always our fault,' says Pamela, drumming her brown fingers on her desk.

'Oh *Pam*. But it *was* Tituba, and she comes right in at the beginning, hoping that Betty isn't going to die,' says Sarah.

'Betty. What about her?' says Rob. 'Little Betty.'

'Oh yeah. Betty. She's the one who starts it all, isn't she?'

'Poor little Betty. She fades away after the first act — and yet she's the one with the real power over them all, even Abigail. This odd little girl who's so frightened when she's caught dancing in the woods that she goes into a trance — or is she just pretending? Look at her when she's alone with Abigail. She comes to her senses suspiciously quickly. She terrifies Abigail, because she drank the blood charm to kill Proctor's wife. The other girls are all older than Betty, maybe they under-estimated her, but she certainly seems to know what was going on.'

'I think she was just frightened of getting into trouble with her father,' says Sarah. 'It was Tituba who started it, telling them about all those Barbados charms.'

'It was Abigail,' says Pamela. 'She's the clever one, she started it all up.'

'Tell you what we'll do,' says Rob. 'None of us know what really happened when the girls all met up in the woods. So let's write our own accounts. We could go back to the diary idea — you could choose to be Abbie, Betty, Tituba — whichever one you like — and write down what really happened.'

'I don't think girls would be able to write in those days,' Sarah says earnestly. 'You did say, Mr Campbell, they weren't properly educated, so I'm not sure they would have kept diaries.'

'Let's *pretend* they did, Sarah,' says Rob.

'Oh Sir, I wish you weren't so keen on all this pre-

139

tending lark,' says Kath. 'It's all right for the brainy-bonces but I can never think what to put. Do we have to do this diary thing? I mean, is it your actual homework or can we just do it if we feel like it?'

'Of course you'll feel like doing it, Kath,' says Rob. 'You're going to want to show me how well you can really write if you put your mind to it — because I don't think you were using very *much* of your mind on this last effort of yours.' He sorts through the pile of papers in his briefcase and waves Kath's in the air. There's large scrawling writing on half a side and that is all.

'Well honestly,' Kath says, joining in the laughter. 'What a subject! Fairy stories. It's daft, isn't it. You can't expect us to think of something to write, not when you want a *fairy* story. We're not five year olds, Sir.'

'It reads like it, Kath,' says Rob. ' "Once upon a time there was a pretty princess and she had lots of pretty dresses and crowns and gold jewellery but she was bored because she didn't have anything to do but one day a handsome prince came along and they fell in love and married and lived happily ever after." Kath!'

'Well. It's got a lot of love interest. And a nice setting. What more do you want?' she giggles.

'Imagination. Style. Narrative pace. Originality. Sophistication,' says Rob, giving Kath her paper and looking through the others. 'Some of you tried really hard. I liked your fairy story about the Grubbits very much, Jane, only I think you and a certain Professor Tolkein might have collaborated occasionally. And Pam, I loved your ogress, I thought she was really great. Read out the cooking pot part, go on.'

Pam reads. I'm in too much of a state to concentrate. He's got my fairy stories there. I can see them in a little wad at the bottom of the pile. What am I going to do if he talks about them in front of everyone? If he makes little jokes? If he wants me to read them out loud? I can't, I won't. I didn't write them for homework, I wrote them for him.

I sit in agony as he gives each girl her work — and

then at last it's me, oh God it's me.

'Well done, May,' Rob says quietly, and he hands me back my stories.

'Right, as we've got a few minutes to spare, let's talk about some of the old fairy stories and see how the budding feminists amongst you might care to interpret them. Which shall we start with? Let's have one with a witch as we've been talking about witchcraft. Do you all know the story of Rapunzel?'

'What about May's stories?' says Kath. 'God, she's written heaps. Aren't you going to get her to read bits out, Sir?'

'I don't want you to be embarrassed, Kath, in case we all start making comparisons,' says Rob. 'Now, Rapunzel. Anyone learning German here? Can you tell us what rapunzel is? It's some kind of vegetable, I think, hot like a radish. Which kind of takes a little of the romance away from the story. It's not quite the same if the Handsome Prince is saying "Oh Radish, Radish, let down your long hair".'

They chuckle, successfully diverted. Under cover of my desk I flip through my fairy stories. He's put lovely little comments in the margins, and at the bottom of the last story he's stuck on seven of those little gold stars you get in Infants School and pencilled *See me.*

When the bell goes I wait until the others are gone.

'You told me to see you, Mr Campbell,' I say demurely.

He looks quickly at the door, and when he sees no-one's looking he gives the end of my nose a little tweak.

'Star pupil,' he says.

'Did you — did you really like them?'

'Oh look at you, lapping up the praise,' says Rob, laughing. 'I didn't think you'd want to read them out in front of all your friends though, is that right?'

'Right.'

'And where's your special pal today?'

'Selina's got glandular fever.'

'Oh dear. My daughter had that last year. It's a

horrible illness, it can go on and on for weeks sometimes.' He looks very concerned. 'They don't seem to
know if it's infectious or not. You're feeling okay, aren't
you, May? I thought you seemed a bit quiet today —
and you're looking very white.'

It's concern for me, for *me*.

'I'm always white. I feel fine.'

'You're sure? Look at you.' He takes hold of my
wrist, gripping it like a handcuff. 'You're so skinny you
look as if you're going to snap any minute. You're not
on a diet, are you?'

'No, of course I'm not.'

'Come round to tea after school and I'll feed you up a
bit. Yes?'

As if I could ever say no.


The child cried. At the darkest hour of the
night, when the whole world seemed hidden
by a huge crow's wing, someone stumbled
upon her. Hands touched her gently,
pausing and stroking whenever she winced.
A flask of ice cold water was held to her
cracked lips and she drank deeply. She was
fed choice berries and nuts and a salad of
strange herbs. Her poor bruised body was
bathed with soft sponges and soothed with
salve. She could not see who her saviour was,
and he did not speak to her, but she knew
her first happiness in his arms.

She struggled to stay awake but her
eyelids grew so heavy she could not stop
them closing. And when she opened them
the sky was blue, the sun was hot, and she
was alone. She moved cautiously. The pain
was gone. She could stand up quite easily.
She leant against the trunk of a tree, trying to
gather her wits, and saw a carving of a heart
etched deep in the bark. She traced the

142

pattern with her finger, and tears ran down her face. She stumbled through the wood, singing the nightingale's song of love and death, happiness and heartbreak. A crow flew overhead but she did not flinch. She was no longer a child. A little black bird could not scare her.

She walked on through the thick forest until she came to the little village at the end where she had once lived. She looked at the ramshackle huts, the stocky men tilling their strips of land, the peasant women stirring their soup, the sturdy children making mudpies. They stared at her, suspicious of this spindly girl with her rags and red hair. A child imitated her song and the villagers sniggered. The girl knew she could never go back to them now. They were her kin folk but she had become a stranger. So she walked on past the village, and the children called names after her, and one boy threw a mud ball that stung her leg and streaked it brown. She washed at the next stream, and the ice cold water reminded her of the secret saviour and she wept again because she thought he was a dream of her delirium, a moon raving sweeter than sanity.

She walked on, singing the nightingale's song with increased yearning. She walked through the country, she walked through the town, until she came to a white palace. There was a Princess within, sighing on a sofa, anxious physicians in attendance. The Princess was plagued with strange pains, and so far they had found no cure. But when the Princess heard the sweet notes of the nightingale's song she sat up, smiling, and then sprang to the window.

'Who is that singing that magical song?

143

Bring them to me immediately. It's so beautiful! It's so sweet it soothes my pain.'

So the girl was taken to the Princess and commanded to keep on singing. She sang willingly enough at first, but after a while her throat ached and her voice faltered.

'Sing up! Sing on! You mustn't stop now,' said the Princess.

The girl sang until her throat was raw. She had a brief respite while the Princess slept, but she was pinched awake at crack of dawn by the irritable royal lady.

'Come along, girl, commence singing. My pain is worse than ever. Quickly now!'

The girl cleared her throat and tried to sing but it was so sore she could only gasp. She whispered an explanation but the Princess seized her by the shoulders and shook her hard.

'Sing! You're to do as I say, don't you understand? What do I care for your pain? What about mine? You are only a poor peasant girl. I am a Princess. So sing up! Sing or you'll be punished, do you hear?'

The Princess's eyes were dark and glittering, her hair long and crow-black. The girl had had enough of punishment. She sang. She sang all day long, she sang until the blood from her sore throat slipped sourly down into her stomach. But her song was not as sweet, the notes were not as pure, the tune not as powerful. So the Princess had her punished all the same. The girl was whipped until she shrieked, and then ordered to sing. She opened her mouth and tried but no sound at all came out.

'I'll teach you to play silly games with me,' said the Princess, rubbing her aching head. 'Throw her into the dungeons. Leave her

144

there until she learns her lesson. Oh yes, after a night in my dungeon you'll soon sing sweetly, my little bird.'

The girl was dragged down to the dungeon and left in the darkest dankest cell. But she was used to such conditions, after a childhood spent in a crow's nest. The night could not frighten her now. She stood on tiptoe, looking through the bars of the narrow window, so she could see the silver moon. She could hear the nightingale's song in her head but she could not sing a note of it with her sore and swollen throat.

She had escaped from one cruel prison only to land in another. She would doubtless languish here, singing until she screamed with pain, screaming with pain until she sang again. Unless ...

Perhaps it was time she tried to rescue herself. She wasn't a silly child any more. She was a grown girl. But still a spindly slip of a girl — spindly enough to slip through the bars of the window. She clasped the bars and swung her legs and squeezed her shoulder through, then her body, her legs and last of all her head. For a few moments it seemed held fast but with one last wrench she was free. She ran through the palace grounds, through the town, through the country, past the peasant village, back to the forest. She knew where she was going.

She ran until she was caught fast in the brambles. She fell to the ground, torn and bleeding. She lay on her back, looking up at the silver moon. She waited — and at last hands touched her gently, pausing and stroking whenever she winced. A flask of ice cold water was held to her cracked lips and she drank deeply. She was fed berries and

145

nuts and a salad of strange herbs. Her poor
bruised body was bathed with soft sponges
and soothed with salve. She could not see
who her saviour was, and he did not speak to
her, but she knew her only happiness was in
his arms. She sang out loud, more sweetly
than ever. She sang and sang and sang.

Her eyelids grew heavy but she pulled a
long hair from her head, threaded it on a
thorn, and stitched her eyelids back against
the bone. Her eyes burned and bled a little,
but she was used to pain by this time. She
had to make sure her eyes stayed open for
ever. You can't miss out on happiness.

# Chapter 18

'Aren't you going to phone your aunt?' Rob asks, when I walk past the telephone box.

I shake my head. I'm not going to. Let her wait and worry. Anyway how can you have a telephone conversation with a person who won't speak?

'How are things at home?' Rob asks casually. 'Is anything the matter?'

'There's always something the matter,' I say, and I smile bravely like Little Orphan Annie.

'Let's go to the cake shop. And I'll need milk and stuff. I went home for the weekend so I haven't got anything in,' says Rob. 'What's your favourite sort of cake? Do you like doughnuts?'

'I love doughnuts.' I pause, trying to catch his exact tone. 'How are things at home?'

He looks taken aback for a moment and then roars with laughter.

'So, so, you cheeky baggage. What sort of doughnuts? Fresh cream? Jam? Rings?'

'I like artificial cream best, actually.' Auntie Win will never buy them, she says they're unwholesome.

'So do I! Those long fat doughnuts with very white cream and scarlet jam — my mouth's watering.'

He buys two each and a big soft sliced loaf and butter and milk and a jar of strawberry jam.

His house seems even darker and shabbier, and the stairs smell so badly of drains or gas or whatever that I stop short, feeling sick.

'What's up?'

'The smell,' I whisper.

He sniffs. 'I suppose it does a bit. Soggy cabbage, is that it?'

'Can't you really smell it?'

'It's just as well, by the look on your face.'

We go into his room and shut the door.

'There. Home Sweet Home. No, not quite. Room Bleak Room is more like it. Does it smell in here too?'

I shake my head politely, but it does.

'I think it does. You're making me nervous,' says Rob, and he opens the window. 'There. Fresh air. Even though we'll freeze.'

'I'm sorry. It's just me. I've got this awfully strong sense of smell. I'm always going on about smells at home. Nan and Auntie Win never seem to notice.'

'They're quite elderly, aren't they? You do lose your sense of smell in time.' He puts the kettle on and bustles about with the tea things.

'I'll do that if you like.'

'No, it's okay, it won't take a minute. May, how old *are* your Aunt and granny? They can still ... cope, can't they?'

'Yes. Well. I suppose so.'

'You don't want to talk about them, do you?'

'Not really.'

'Okay. God, these doughnuts are huge. You are going to eat two, aren't you? Join me in the sinful glut?'

'Yes please.'

'And strawberry jam sandwiches. On wicked white bread. Sal would absolutely do her nut if she could see this meal.'

Sal. His wife.

'Is she — Sal — into health foods then?'

'You bet. Brown bread so coarse you get little bits of combine harvester in every bite, gritty honey, no cake at all. Tea is not a treat in our household. Emily used to do Cookery at school and that was great — I remember she once did this amazing Millionaire pudding thing —

148

now, how can I describe it?'

'Chocolate toffee fudge on shortbread?'

'Yes!'

'I can make that.'

'Really? You are a girl of amazing talents.'

'I could make you some if you like.'

'*Would* you? I'd give anything for Millionaire pudding. Great slabs of it.'

'Won't Emily make you some?'

'She's not into Cookery now. Or treats for Daddy.'

'What is she into?'

'God knows. Boys. Loud music. Tarty clothes. Parties. Drink. Cigarettes. She hasn't quite got to the head-in-a-bag-of-Evostick stage but give her time.'

'And she's younger than me?'

'Nearly fourteen.'

'And she smokes and drinks?'

'Well. A little. To impress her friends. And depress me.'

'What does she look like? Is she pretty?'

'She used to be. She still looks lovely early in the morning in her dressing gown with her hair all rumpled and no make up. She looks like my little girl then. Only she doesn't seem to want to be my Emily any more.' He bites his doughnut and then licks sugar from his fingertips, sighing. 'Shut me up, May, I'm starting to get maudlin. Let's talk about you and your amazing fairy stories. What are we going to do with them? I keep scouring the papers for children's writing competitions because I'm sure you'd win, hands down.'

'No I wouldn't. They're babyish really. Fairy stories.'

'Don't listen to silly old Kath. And there's nothing babyish about those stories. Tell me, do you deliberately make them symbolic, or do they just come out that way?'

'I'm–I'm not sure.'

'How long does it take you to write them?'

'I don't know. Not very long. Well, the first one did, but now I've sort of got the hang of them.'

'Have you read a lot of fairy stories yourself?'

'Not really. Grandad used to make up stories for me when I was very little, but I don't think he got them out of a book.'

I'd forgotten Grandad's stories up until now. It was before I started school. I used to sit on his foot and he'd give me rides up and down in the air — I must have been about three or four — and then when he got tired or I started squealing too loudly he'd pull me up onto his knee and tell me a story while I played with his pocket watch. What's happened to his watch? Nan wanted Grandad cremated in his best suit. Did she take the watch out of his pocket? Or did it blacken and burn like Grandad?

'You obviously loved him a lot,' Rob says softly.

'Mm. You don't think — I know he worried about me a lot and — he died of a heart attack, you see, and that's caused by worry, isn't it, so you don't think it could have been — well, my fault?'

'No!' He looks outraged. 'Whoever gave you that idea?'

'No-one. It was just — well I once stayed out late and Grandad got angina — and then there was my portrait of him, I–I . . .'

'Of course his heart attack wasn't your fault. He was an old man, May. His heart was probably worn out.'

'Yes, but I — when I painted him, I . . .'

'Listen to me. If people had heart attacks worrying about their children — or grandchildren — then I'd have keeled over long ago. Emily stayed out all night at a party at Christmas and Sal and I just about went demented, but we didn't have heart attacks. And if we *had* it wouldn't have been Emily's fault. It would have been because of furred up arteries in the heart, dodgy valves or whatever — you probably know more about it than me, I wasn't that great at Biology. You must believe me, May.'

He's kneeling in front of me, looking straight in my eyes. I can't believe him but I don't care. I want us to

150

stay as close as this for ever. I'm not even thinking about Grandad now. It's just Rob and me. I want him to kiss me. Why won't he kiss me? I stare at him imploringly, opening my eyes wide so that they start stinging a little. I can easily make them water. I feel the tears dribbling down my cheeks.

'Don't be sad, you poor little love,' says Rob, and he reaches out and I think he's going to take me in his arms at last. But he just pats my shoulder a little awkwardly.

'There now. Don't cry. Please don't. You'll make me start too, if you don't watch out.'

'You?' I stare up at him. 'Why?'

'Oh. Because I'm feeling a bit down at the moment. I had a lousy weekend and — I don't know, everything seems to have got on top of me. I can't see where I'm going any more.' He stops patting. 'See! You've got me started now. Let's have a strawberry jam sandwich and then I might shut up.'

'I think you'd feel better if you did talk about it.'

I'm serious but he laughs at me and calls me little Agony Auntie May. Then he sees he's hurt my feelings and he looks guilty.

'You're being very sweet and kind and concerned. I'm sorry.'

'Is it Emily worrying you? Did she go to another party at the weekend?'

'No, she just went out with her friends. She was okay I suppose.'

'So was it ... Sal?'

'I suppose so. We had a row. Which I see now was only to be expected. It was stupid of me to think things would be different. I mean, I knew we weren't really close any more. That was one of the reasons why I applied for this writing job. So we could have six months apart, have a break from each other to try to work out what we want from our relationship. Only it looks as if the break might be permanent now.'

'And you don't want it to be?'

'I don't know what I want any more.'

I know what I want. I want him.

'I know one thing though.'

'What?'

'I don't half miss her.'

'Sal?'

'Emily. We used to be so close. I looked after her when she was little. I gave up working for this stupid woman's magazine and stayed at home writing free-lance while Sal went back to work. I didn't get much writing done, I just played with Emily. I'd crawl into her Wendy House with her and play with all her dolls and teddies and I'd read to her and draw funny pictures for her — and then we'd go out to the swings and we'd feed the ducks or have a picnic in the park. I used to buy doughnuts just like today and Emily would stuff herself and then not want her supper and — do shut me up, May. This must be boring for you. Emily can't stand it when I twitter on about the past.'

'She must miss you too.'

'I don't think so. She's still mildly fond of me, but I've become a sloppy embarrassment. She's grown out of me. It's much better for both of us. I think we were really too close when she was little. It was my fault. I probably made far too many emotional demands on her. No wonder poor old Em needs to rebel a bit now.'

'I think you sound as if you were a wonderful father.'

'Oh May.'

'I mean it. I'd have given anything to have a father like you.'

He takes hold of my hand.

'What about your father then?'

I shrug. I don't say anything. He squeezes my hand. I want him to hold it for ever and ever. He moves his fingers. He's trying to get away. I hold on. He looks at me and laughs. I laugh to. He's turning it into a game but we both know it's serious.

We are holding hands like the couple in my painting. My spell is working.

# Chapter 19

'I want a word with you, young lady.'

Auntie Win marches into my bedroom.

'How can you have a word when you're not speaking to me?'

Auntie Win flushes and rubs her cheeks with the back of her hands as if she's trying to smooth the colour away. She takes several deep breaths, composing herself. She fingers the books on my shelf and then finds the photograph of Amy. She picks it up and dusts it with the sleeve of her cardigan.

'What would your mother say if she could hear you talking like that?' she says sadly.

'She's dead.'

'I often think she's still with us, May. I think she's watching over you — and I think she must be very unhappy now.'

'I hate it when you talk about her like that.'

'Of course you do. When you've got a guilty conscience.'

'I haven't.'

'Well, you jolly well should have, you naughty girl. Nan and I have been worrying ourselves sick over you.' She stops dusting the photo and peers at it. 'What's this orange stuff on the glass? It's not paint, is it?'

I don't answer.

'What have you been doing to this photograph? The glass is all smeared and scratched. Your mother's photograph!'

'Look, I don't really want it any more. You have it if it means so much to you.'

'I think we'll have to get another sheet of glass. I don't know what you've been up to. I'll take it in to the glass shop tomorrow, see if they can cut me a piece the right size.'

'I don't *want* it.'

'You don't want your own mother. Is that it?'

'Yes. That's it.'

Auntie Win shakes her head sorrowfully.

'I never thought I'd live to hear you say that.'

'She's dead. She died nearly fifteen years ago. I never even knew her.'

'She took you in her arms, May. Weak as she was, she took you in her arms and she kissed your little head and —'

'You're making all that up! How on earth do you know? You weren't there in the hospital with her, were you? So you don't know a thing about it.'

'Lower your voice, please. I won't have you using that shrill tone.'

'Please, I've got all this homework to do, couldn't I just get on with it?'

'So why did you stay out until six o'clock, tell me that, Madam?'

'Six o'clock! This is barmy. Most of my friends stay out till *twelve* o'clock, no bother at all. But all right, you're angry because I didn't phone, although how I could phone when you weren't even speaking to me I don't know, but *anyway*, can't you just tell me off? Punish me. Do what you like. Only don't keep bringing my mother into it, it's so *sick.*'

'Sick! To love your mother? You're the one who's sick, May. Sick in the head. Your Nannie feels we should get the doctor to you and I think she may be right.'

'Nan's the one that's going off her head, not me. She doesn't even remember about Grandad half the time. And you're mad too, going on and on about *her* all the

154

time. Why does she mean so much to you? She wasn't your daughter, she was only your niece.'

'You don't know what you're talking about,' says Auntie Win. She's got tears in her eyes and I'm suddenly sorry. I want to tell her I'm sorry, I want to stop hurting her, I want to go back to being the meek little May who's no trouble at all. But I can't climb back into that May, it was too tight a fit, all the life was being squeezed out of me. I could make that a fairy tale, a little peasant girl who is given a magic silver gown by a King and Queen still grieving for their lost princess and inside the silver gown the peasant girl does her best to shine and sparkle, but she's not the lost princess, she's only a little peasant girl and she keeps forgetting her manners and playing in the pig-pens and the potato patch so that the silver gown gets torn and tarnished and as she grows older it gets tighter and tighter until it cuts right into her flesh like a bacon slicer but still she doesn't dare take it off until . . .

'Perhaps it's time you and I had a serious talk, May.'

'No. I don't want to. No, I'm sorry. Please just leave me alone.' I stand up and push past her, out of my bedroom.

I run downstairs and into the living room. The television is blaring but Nan is fast asleep, nodding on the sofa with her legs sagging open and her skirt riding up. I gently push her skirt down until she's decent and then carefully sit beside her, cautiously lolling until my head touches her shoulder. I don't want to wake her, I just want to sit here with her and pretend that everything is all right, that my Grannie and I are watching television together. But Nan starts and mumbles and opens her eyes. She blinks at me, surprised, and then smiles because she's forgotten I'm in disgrace.

'Hello, pet. Come to watch *Coronation Street*, have you?'

*Coronation Street* has been on and gone but Nan still seems to think she's watching it. She nods and smiles at some new comedy programme and talks to the screen.

'Come on, now, we've got a bit sick of you. Let's go and have a look at Elsie Tanner's new fancy man. Or what about old Ena Sharples, she's always a scream.'

'They're not in it any more, Nan. They haven't been for donkey's years. And anyway, this isn't *Coronation Street*, can't you see?'

'Isn't it, dear?' Nan says, not at all put out.

'Perhaps you need new glasses.'

'My glasses?' Nan takes them off and looks at them. They're not even her glasses. They're an old reading pair of Grandad's. Nan realises this and giggles.

'Whoops! I've only gone and put on your Grandad's glasses. Dearie me, aren't I silly. Go and give these to your Grandad, pet, and see if you can find my own specs.'

I hesitate and then I find Nan's own glasses at the bottom of her handbag, all higgledy piggledy in a mess of damp hankies and broken combs and toffee wrappers. I do my best to clean them and then I offer them to Nan. She puts them on.

'That's better,' she says politely, although they're still so smeared I don't think she can see much at all.

I hesitate. Then I dare say it.

'Nan, Grandad's dead. Don't you remember?'

She watches the television screen, not reacting.

'Nan.' I raise my voice. 'Nan, Grandad's *dead*.'

Nan still watches television, but she's frowning.

'Don't shout, dear. You've been rather a rude girl recently. We've been a bit upset about it, Auntie Win and me.'

So she's remembered that.

'Auntie Win says you think I ought to see a doctor.'

'Yes, dear. Just for a check up. I'm sure he'll say it's just your age. You know.' She lowers her voice. 'Your monthlies.'

'It can't be my periods, Nan, I haven't started yet.'

I'm the only girl in our class. Even the babies in the first year use the end lavatory with the special sanitary towel machine. I am sure I am never going to start.

156

That would make a good fairy story too. A changeling child who doesn't change.

'May dear, don't sit there with that sulky face. Why won't you answer? You don't want to upset your old Nannie, do you?'

'Sorry, Nan. I didn't hear. What did you say?'

Nan puts her head on one side.

'I can't remember!' she says. 'Dear oh dear. I'm getting so forgetful now. I'll forget my own head next.' She tries to laugh but her eyes are anxious behind her smeared glasses. I picture Nan groping round the living room, a grisly stump protruding from her crotcheted collar, while her head is left on the sofa, skewered on her knitting needles like a big bag of wool. Perhaps I am mad after all. And Nan. And Auntie Win. Perhaps we are all cursed with the same madness. No, I am the only one who can curse. I am the witch. It is obviously mad to believe I am a witch. But if that's the case then Selina is mad too.

Nan forgets that she is forgetful, watches her own twenty year old version of *Coronation Street* on the television, and falls asleep. I try to watch the real programme but I can't concentrate on it any more than Nan. Selina stares at me from the screen, her eyes glittering.

I shall have to go round to see her. She is still ill. Is glandular fever serious? I think of those big lumps on her neck and instantly the screen Selina bubbles with boils, her neck ballooning. The pulses in my own neck tick like a clock.

They tick all night and the next day I don't set off for school, I go to see Selina instead. The pulses tick and tock madly, and alarm rings in my head. I don't know why I'm so scared. She can't do me any harm. Although it all started when I stepped into that silver pentacle on Twelfth Night. But it wasn't a real pentacle, it was just a string of tinsel. And Selina's witchcraft is all pretend too, a silly superstitious game.

Selina's mother opens the door. She couldn't be any-

157

one else. And she *is* a witch.

'Mrs Murray?'

'Yes, sweetie?' Her hair is even longer and blacker than Selina's, swirling over her shoulders like a cloak. Her eyes gleam, heavily outlined with kohl. They are very dark and her face is deathly pale. She's wearing a black velvet smock with huge gathered sleeves, black trousers and silver high-heeled slippers. She has matching silver varnish on her fingernails and an elaborate ring on every finger.

'I just wondered if Selina's all right,' I mutter.

'Ah! Are you one of Selina's friends from school? Do come in, darling. Poor Selina's not very well at all. She's got glandular fever, isn't it a bore? She's going to be off school for a while.' She ushers me in and stands smiling at me in the hall. 'What year are you in, mmm?'

'The fourth.'

'Of course!' she says quickly 'Well, come and see the invalid.'

'I can't really stay, I just —'

'Don't worry, I don't think she's horribly infectious — although we could fashion you a little surgical mask out of a scarf, that might be fun.'

'No, really, it's —'

Well, what is it? How can I say I'm frightened of Selina herself, not her germs. I can't say it so I trudge glumly up the stairs after Mrs Murray. She walks like Selina. She could be her from the back, although her bottom is quite a bit bigger. Her smock is several inches too short. And close up I can see her face is lined under her white make-up and her hair is too black to be true, she must dye it now. She is a sad old shadow of Selina's beauty. Whereas I am the sad young shade of my mother. Although would Amy still be young and beautiful if she were alive now? She'd be thirty-five, that's almost middle-aged. Maybe she'd have put on a bit of weight too. Could she even have a big bottom? And what about her hair? People don't stay blonde forever. Would she have to keep touching up her roots with peroxide?

158

It's such an exhilarating idea that I bounce into Selina's room with a smile on my face.

'Oh Christ. Not you again,' says Selina.

'That's not a very charming way to greet your guest,' says Mrs Murray, putting her arm round me. 'Take no notice of her, darling. She's not feeling very well and Selina is always an utter pain when she's poorly. I'll fix you both a drink.'

'Go *away*,' says Selina, and she plugs herself into her Walkman and shuts her eyes.

Mrs Murray sighs and raises her eyebrows at me. 'I'll get those drinks. Let's hope it chokes Selina, hm?'

I like Mrs Murray. I think I like her much more than Selina. She leaves us alone although her musky perfume lingers. Selina hunches down in her bed with her headphones on, not even looking at me.

'How do you feel?' I ask loudly.

If she heard me she obviously doesn't think it worth an answer.

I glance at the ceiling. She's scraped the silver paper moon away. Perhaps it wasn't ever there. Perhaps I am even madder than I think and I imagined the whole thing. But Selina's eyes flicker upwards too and I know she knows what I'm looking for. There's a hint of a smile on her lips.

'Selina.' I sit down on her bed and give a timid tug at her headphones.

'Do you mind? And get off the bed. I ache everywhere. I don't want you sprawling all over me.'

'Quick, Selina, before your mother comes back. How did you get on with Ben and Pete on Saturday?'

'You should have stayed if you're so interested.'

'I couldn't, you know I couldn't. I got into terrible trouble with my aunt as it was. Did Ben and Pete stay a long time? What did you do?'

'Oh we had a good laugh. About you, mostly.'

'Don't be like that, please. Look, I did come at the weekend, and I've come round now. What more do you want? We had such fun until those boys turned up.

159

Selina — you didn't tell them about me running round the willow tree, did you?'

'That was the biggest laugh of all,' says Selina.

I'm wasting my time. I stay and sip the weird weak tea Mrs Murray brings but Selina's so uncommunicative there's not really any point. I want to tell her about Rob. I want to tell her about him so badly so she'll stop treating me with contempt. I know she'd sit up and listen if I told her I'd been to his flat. She'd go emerald green with envy. But I'm not going to tell her. I'm not that much of a fool.

'I'm going now,' I say, and I walk out of the room without waiting to see if she'll reply.

Mrs Murray hears me in the hall.

'Oh dear, are you going already, sweetie? Has that horrid girl been mean to you?'

'No, not really.'

'That means yes. Don't take it to heart, she's being beastly to everyone. It's not just the glandular fever. She's been very fed up since Christmas when Bruno told her he didn't want to see her any more.'

'Bruno said ...?'

'Well, it was obvious when he started at Warwick he was going to lose interest in Selina. He was fond of her, of course, but she's so much younger. As soon as he started going round with the other students, well ...'

I nod wisely.

'Poor Selina. Still that doesn't excuse her being rude to her friends, especially when you've come round specially to see her.'

'Oh well. I'd better get off to school now, I'll be ever so late.' I hand her my teacup. 'Thank you very much for the tea, Mrs Murray.'

'You didn't finish it. Didn't you like it?'

'It's lovely, it's just ... *Is* it tea?'

'Herbal tea. It's very good for you. But it's possibly an acquired taste. Don't look too worried, it's not poison, I promise.'

I stare at her and wonder whether I dare ask her

160

outright. Excuse me, Mrs Murray, but would you mind telling me if you're a witch? Only I can't ask outright. I try to be devious.

'Did you enjoy your weekend away?'

She looks surprised.

'Yes, sweetie, it was great fun.'

'Was it ... Selina said it was a conference?'

'That's right, in Wales. The land of our fathers. Or mother, in my case. Yes dear, it was a magical weekend,' says Mrs Murray, and she smiles Selina's smile.

# Chapter 20

'Hello ... Robin.'

It's the first time I've dared to use his first name. I can feel my cheeks burning. He's going red too. I can't believe it. I've made him blush.

'Hello May.' He sounds casual enough. Perhaps he's just hot. Although it's so cold I'm shivering. I've been waiting in the playground for him for ages.

He's looking over his shoulder, glancing at the gate. I think he's making sure it's safe. It is safe, everyone else has gone home.

'Have you got any more stories for me?' he asks.

'No. But I have got something. A surprise.'

'What?' he says, sounding cautious.

I was going to wait until we were back in his flat but I suppose it won't matter if I give it to him now. I fish in my schoolbag for the packet.

'Here you are.'

He takes the packet and peers inside it. He looks surprised.

'Thank you very much.'

Auntie Win wouldn't let me make Millionaire's pudding even though I begged her. She said we couldn't afford fancy ingredients, and she didn't want me making elaborate cakes in her kitchen. I think she was just saying it to spite me. I waited until she'd gone to bed and then I crept into the kitchen and made shortbread. She surely can't begrudge me a bit of butter and sugar.

But it's no use, it doesn't look as if he likes it.

'I'm sorry it's not Millionaire's pudding,' I say miserably. 'Don't you like shortbread?'

'Oh I do. It's my favourite. Yes, I love it.'

'It's like Millionaire's pudding — without the butterscotch and the chocolate. So it's a sort of Pauper's pudding.'

I've rehearsed this little joke. It makes him laugh. He's laughing almost too much, on and on. What's wrong, what's *wrong*?'

'It's very kind of you, May,' he says when he's stopped laughing at last.

And then there's a gap in the conversation. We stand opposite each other, our eyes flickering in and out of contact.

'You're shivering,' says Rob. 'Hadn't you better —'

'What?'

'Won't your Auntie and ... Won't they be wondering what's happend to you?'

'No. They think I'm doing Art. So I can come back with you.'

'Oh. Well.'

'What's the matter?'

'Nothing. Nothing at all. Come on then.'

'You seem a bit funny.'

'No, I'm fine.'

He wraps his red scarf round his neck and we start off. He looks round again as we go out the gate.

'There is something wrong.'

'No, there's not. I'm just a bit — I'm not sure this writer in residence thing is working out, that's part of it. It's such a silly thing. I'm not a schoolteacher, I'm not a friend, I just don't know how to relate to everyone.'

'In what way?'

'In any way. It's so difficult. And I've got to be so careful.' He stops walking and looks at me. 'You see, I was talking to one of the teachers in the staffroom today and ...'

I wait.

163

He looks away.

'Oh it's all so stupid,' he mutters.

'What's stupid?'

'Girl's schools.'

'Why?'

'Just because. I don't know. I feel I'm out of my depth. I don't seem to be getting through to anyone.'

'You're getting through to me.'

'Oh May. Stop being so nice to me. And you must admit, the others don't seem to be getting anything out of my writing class even if you are.'

'You mustn't mind them. They're not interested in writing.'

'Quite! It's my job to interest them, isn't it? And I'm not doing it. I should never have got started on *The Crucible*, it isn't working at all. And the fairy stories weren't much of a success either — apart from yours. I think I should have stuck to the diary theme, maybe that would have worked better. That first lesson seemed okay, didn't it?'

'They've all been fine, really.'

I don't see why he's getting so worried about it. The girls are much better behaved in his lesson than most of the others. It isn't because of what he says and does. It's because they think he's cute. Some of them have got a crush on him. But none of them care about him the way I do. He's mine. He's *mine*. I've cast the spells, I've made him mine.

'What do you really think, May?' he asks. 'Should I have stuck to the diary idea?'

'Maybe. Then you could read them extracts from *The Misfit*. They'd like that.'

'You're an old flatterer,' he says, laughing properly this time.

'No I'm not, I mean it. I think it's a wonderful book. And I think Mark is so real.'

'Good.'

'I like him so much.'

He hesitates.

164

'Oh May. Look. I don't think —' He closes his eyes for a moment and then looks straight at me. 'I think you'd better run off home now.'

'But —'

'I know it's stupid, but I don't think you really ought to come back to my flat.'

'Why? What have I done?'

'You haven't done anything, you silly girl. It's just — maybe your Aunt wouldn't really like it.'

'I *told* you —'

'And it's probably not very sensible'

'What do you mean?'

'Well, I happened to mention in the staffroom that you'd come round to tea and this other teacher seemed to think it wasn't a very sensible idea.'

'You told someone?'

'Well, of course. I mean, it wasn't a secret.'

Of course it was a secret. I can't bear it. He can't care. The spell isn't working after all.

'Come on, now, May, no need to look so tragic. Look, we can still be friends. May, *please.*'

But I don't want to please him any more. I turn and run away, leaving him calling after me, clutching his greasy paper bag of shortbread. I run all the way home and lock myself into the bathroom, the only place Auntie Win can't barge in on me. Rob's words are burning so fiercely inside me that I can't quench them, not even when I lie down on the cold lino floor.

How can we still be friends? I don't want to be friends with him now. I don't need him.

But I feel so empty without him.

I get up, I go to school, I do my lessons, I go home, I eat, I do my homework, I draw my curtains and I go to bed. It's as if I'm only a shadow of a person.

That's the way people treat me. As if I don't exist in my own right. Nan and Auntie Win are still barely speaking to me. Well, Nan's all right when she's awake, I suppose, but she's nearly always asleep nowadays. And the pills she's taking make her seem so dozy even

165

when she's pottering about the house. She sometimes forgets and calls me Amy and it makes me feel more of a shadow than ever.

Auntie Win knows who I am all right. She's made it plain what she thinks of me. I hear her crying at night. I try to burrow away from the sound under the covers, but every time I put my head out I can still hear her sobbing. I can't stand looking at her at breakfast time. Her eyelids swell like sponges.

I gulp down my cornflakes in two minutes and run away from her. I get to school earlier and earlier.

And then one morning Selina is back. I stare at her. She still looks ill. She's very pale and there are dark shadows like bruises under her eyes.

'Selina!'

'Don't sound so surprised.'

'Are you better?'

'I suppose so.' She sighs and walks to her desk. I follow her and stand, hovering.

'I'm glad you're back.'

'I'm not.'

'Are you very fed up?'

'Mmm.'

'I am too.'

'Oh yeah?' says Selina. She stares down at her desk. There's a name inked on the top in her neat italic handwriting. Bruno. She suddenly spits on her finger and rubs at it. Bruno blotches and becomes a blue smudge.

'It's all over with Bruno, isn't it?' I whisper.

'What? Of course not,' Selina insists furiously. 'Bruno and I —'

'Your mother told me,' I interrupt.

'She *told* you?' Selina's hand clenches into a fist and she bangs the desk.

'Don't be cross. I won't tell anyone, not if you don't want me to.'

'I can't stand it, May,' Selina says, and there are tears in her dark eyes. 'He was home at the weekend and he came round when he heard I was ill and he was so sweet to me — and I thought — but he was just messing me around. He's got this other girl at Warwick. He just wants to be *friends* with me.'

'That's what they always want, isn't it?' I say bitterly.

'How would you know?' says Selina, but she's not really cross any more. She leans against me. 'Oh May. I don't know what I'm going to do. It's so awful without him.'

'What about Ben? Or Pete?'

'Do me a favour!'

'They seemed awfully keen on you.'

'Well I can't stick them.'

'Then why did you let them in?'

'I said, didn't I? I wanted a bit of a laugh.'

'A laugh at me,' I say, and I push her away.

'No, not you. Honestly May, I didn't tell them a thing. As if I would. You're right, I should have chucked them straight out. We were having a much better time by ourselves.' She pulls me back. Her head is very close to mine. 'Weren't we, sister witch?'

'We were,' I whisper. 'Selina, why don't *you* run round the willow tree widdershins? Then you could maybe charm Bruno back if you really want him so badly.'

'Maybe I will,' says Selina. She sits up straight, her eyes glittering. 'Or maybe I'll try something else. Something a little stronger than a love charm.'

My heart starts thudding.

'What a good idea,' says Selina. 'You'll help me, won't you, May?'

'I didn't mean ... I don't think I want to.'

'You've got to. You're my secret sister. You can't back out now. It's time we evoked the power of the shade.'

167

# Chapter 21

Selina takes her time answering her door. Her hands slip on the catch and she holds them out in front of her awkwardly, as if they belong to someone else. They certainly don't look like Selina's hands any more. They are twice their usual size, pale and puffy.

'What's the matter? What are you doing?'

'I'm making jam tarts,' says Selina, walking back to the kitchen.

I follow her and see that she's not joking. She plunges her hands back into a huge bowl of dough and kneads it energetically, making the spoons and jars and tins on the table vibrate like a tiny percussion band.

I watch her silently, feeling so angry. She begged me to come round to her house on Saturday afternoon. She insisted it was the only possible time she could make sure both her parents would be out (her father playing golf, her mother telling fortunes). I had to endure another scene with Auntie Win before I could get out myself. I went through with it because Selina swore she had to have my help. And yet she doesn't need me to prance about like the Queen of Hearts, making her tarts.

'I suppose you're not bothered about Bruno now,' I say sourly.

'What?' Selina pauses and tries to push her hair out of her eyes with her pastry cutter. 'Of course I am! That's why I'm making all these fiddly little tarts.'

'How many are you making? You'll have heaps.'

'It's not all for tarts, stupid. They're just the camouflage. Oh my wretched hair, look, can you tuck it behind my ear, May?'

I try to anchor it out of harm's way although there doesn't seem to be much point now.

'It's like one of those 18th century powdered wigs,' I say. 'What camouflage?'

'This dough looks a bit odd, doesn't it? It won't go smooth. Still, it doesn't matter, I'm not trying to win a cookery prize. Which is just as well. Remember when we did Home Economics in the first year and I spilled my strawberry shape into Mrs Henchard's lap?' Selina sniggers and twists her great ball of dough in half.

'Here, May. Get your coat off and help. I'll make the tarts with this bit. This other piece is yours. I want you to make me an image.'

I blink at her.

'Come on, get ready,' Selina hisses. Then she composes her face and stands still, pale and serious. She raises her arms above her head and looks upwards.

'Grant your earthly daughter May the power of the shade, Great Goddess of the Silver Moon,' she cries. She turns her head and frowns at me. 'Pray for the power yourself, then.'

'I don't know what to say,' I mumble. 'I don't know what you mean anyway. What sort of image?'

'I want you to make an image of Bruno. A little dough boy Bruno, okay? And we'll bake it and then when it's hot and still soft from the oven we'll stick pins in it,' says Selina.

'You're not serious?'

'You bet I am. He sent me a chatty little card this morning. So bright and matey. Hopes I'm much better now. Having a ball. Oh and he is too. He and this stupid bitch he thinks he's in love with. Well, I'll show him. I'll make him love *me*.'

'You're going to stick pins in him?'

'Not *him*, you idiot. His image. To give him a little pain, a little pang of love. And perhaps his eyes will prick a little with tears of regret. His stomach clench a

169

little with apprehension. His limbs shake a little with hopeless longing. Just a little, just a little, just a little,' Selina croons.

'It won't really hurt him, will it?' I say uneasily.

'Just a *little*,' says Selina, and she smiles. 'Come *on*, my mother will be back by five. So raise your arms and ask for the power.'

'Why don't you do it with her if she's a witch.'

'It's none of her business, Bruno and me. And anyway, she wouldn't approve of me using the power of the shade. She doesn't think I've attained the appropriate degree of knowledge.'

'Well I certainly haven't. I don't see why I have to get involved. It's none of my business either.'

'But I'm hopeless at art, you know I am. How can I make a dough Bruno? It's got to *look* like him. Please help me, sister. I can't do it without you.'

'Well ... I'm not doing any of the pin bit.'

'You don't have to. You can leave that to me. Make me an image, that's all I want. Please May. Just so that he suffers a little bit. So he knows what it's been like for me. I don't know why you don't want to help me, May. I didn't think you liked boys.'

'I don't. Or men. All right. I'll make this image.'

I roll up my sleeves and powder my hands with flour. I try to remember what Bruno looks like. As I think my fingers start fashioning a little figure out of the dough. Selina watches me intently. Her gaze is so unnerving that my fingers fumble.

'Don't keep staring at me. Can't you get on with making your jam tarts?'

'Sh! I'm willing the powers of the shade. And you should be doing it too. Pray to the Moon Goddess, May. Invoke all the demons from the dark side of the moon, the waning spirits who delight in the skills of the shadows.'

She keeps up this manic muttering as I work. I make a slender body and style a suit out of the dough. I take a fork and line little pin-stripes onto the trousers and jacket. I make sure the waistcoat shows, swirling my fork to make a pattern like brocade. The feet are easy, pale dough plimsolls. I fold two hands upon his waistcoated chest. And now there's just the head. I comb his hair with my fork, making it stand up in spikes. Now the face. It's a kind face, with a sweet smile. Bruno was kind to me.

'I don't want to hurt him.'

'*I'll* do the pins, I said. Here May, that's brilliant. It's just like him.'

'It's too like him. I don't want to do it any more. It's getting too real.' I look at the dough image. The eyes are staring. The body is stiff and still. 'Oh God, he looks dead,' I wail, and I'm about to scrunch up the dough, but Selina catches my hands.

'Leave it! It's perfect. Come on, help me edge him onto the baking tray.'

'No, please, I don't want to.'

'We can't stop now. You can never stop, not when you've started,' says Selina, carefully picking Bruno up and laying him on the tray. 'There! He doesn't look a bit dead, May. Wave to her, Bruno, go on.' She takes his pastry arm and shakes it. He gives me a limp salute. 'There! See. Now, let's tuck you up, Bruno, my boy. That's it. Lie still. You feel a bit cold to me. We'll soon warm you up, eh? Just wait one second while I finish my tarts.'

'He won't really suffer, will he, Selina?' I ask her anxiously, as she fills her tarts with jam.

'He will suffer as I have suffered. Or maybe just a little bit more,' says Selina. 'Come on, help me with these tarts or we'll never get done.'

The strawberry jam is scarlet, like blood. I stare at the white dough, the red jam, feeling sick.

'But he won't — you're not really going to *harm* him?'

'Harm him? I love him, don't I?' says Selina, and she stoops and kisses his small pastry smile.

'Bake well, Bruno beloved,' she says, and she thrusts

the tin of tarts and the baking tray inside the oven. She bangs the door on him quickly, as if she's scared he'll escape.

'You're just like a witch in a fairy story,' I say, my arm prickling. 'You know, Hansel and Gretel and the witch has this gingerbread house with barley sugar windows.'

'It must have got very sticky in the summer,' says Selina. 'Don't start going on about those boring old fairy tales, you're worse than Robin Campbell. Where did you find those ones you copied out for him?'

'I didn't copy them. I made them up myself.'

'Really? What a waste of time!'

'Shall we clear up the kitchen while the — the tarts are cooking?'

'No. I can't be bothered. It's so hot in here.' Selina washes her hands under the cold tap. She dries them and then sees she's still got pastry under her long nails. She sighs impatiently and washes her hands all over again, with hot water and a lot of soap. I can't help thinking about Lady Macbeth.

We go into the great white living room and loll there uneasily. Selina keeps looking at her watch.

'We spent ages messing about making the things. It's nearly four o'clock.'

'Your mother isn't due back till five, you said.'

'Yes, but she could come back sooner. Although she is usually ages at Marie's. Marie Holmwood, you know, the actress.' Selina sighs at my blank expression. 'Well, everyone else in the whole world has heard of Marie Holmwood. She gets my mother to tell her fortune once a quarter, sometimes even once a month. Lots of people in the film and television world consult my mother, they all think she's wonderful.'

'But if she can really tell fortunes won't she be able to work out what you've been doing? Won't she gaze into her crystal ball or whatever and see what you're doing to Bruno?' I'm not really serious but Selina looks worried.

'I don't think she could,' she says, fiddling with her hair. There are still streaks of flour in it, and I try to pat them away for her. Selina gets a hairbrush and I untie her hair and brush it all out for her. I know how to brush properly because of my own long hair. I do it slowly and rhythmically from the roots right down almost to the ends. Selina shivers.

'That feels lovely. Do you think my mother might read it in the cards?'

'No, of course not. She's not telling your fortune, is she?'

'I suppose not.' She sniffs. 'I can smell the things cooking. May —'

I wait.

'He is asking for it, isn't he? He said he loved me. He said all sorts of things. He made me believe … And yet now he's treating me as if I'm some silly little kid.'

'I know,' I say softly, winding a strand of her hair round my finger.

'And what hurts the most — he's told this girl of his all about me.'

'You can't trust any of them,' I say, and I brush her hair back behind her ears. They stick out very slightly, a small comical mar to her beauty. I suddenly feel so close to her I want to tell her all my secrets too. I open my mouth, my tongue ready to roll an R, but Selina is sniffing the air.

'They smell as if they're ready. We mustn't let it get too hard. Come on, let's go and see.'

We both hesitate in front of the oven.

'Go on. Open it, May. We don't want them to burn,' says Selina, starting to fill the basin with hot water, flinging the dishes about.

'You open it.'

'For God's sake, I'm doing the washing up. I can't do everything,' says Selina, but then she seizes a towel and walks over to the oven. 'Okay, okay, *I'll* do it,' she says, and she opens the door with a brave flourish.

We take no notice of the tarts. We only have eyes for

173

Bruno. The baking has bloated him horribly. His smile has slipped, his stomach swollen, his suit has split at the seams.

'What's *happened* to him?'

'Self-raising flour,' Selina says shakily. 'We forgot it would rise and spread a bit. He's old Billy Bunter Bruno now.'

'He looks as if he's been eating all the jam tarts.'

We both start giggling, clutching each other.

'Come on. We'd better get on with it,' Selina gasps. She gives the bloated Bruno a tentative poke in the tummy. It moves, almost as if he were breathing. Our giggles become hysterical. 'Right. Up in my room. I've got everything ready.'

She puts on a pair of oven gloves, seizes the baking tray, and bears it aloft. I follow behind, still giggling. The whole ceremony has become a farce. That's what it is, a silly play. Sticking pins in a dough model can't really hurt Bruno. It doesn't even look like Bruno any more. It's all an elaborate game to make Selina feel better.

But it doesn't seem like a game up in the bedroom. The silver moon shines down on the candles arranged round the pentacle. The box of pins is waiting on a little black velvet cushion.

Selina pulls her long robe on over her jeans and hands me her white nightdress. I put it on obediently. Selina places the baking tray inside the pentacle and then we step inside too. It doesn't leave much room and we jostle together as we kneel, but neither of us giggle now.

Selina looks up at the silver moon.

'We beseech your help, oh Great Silver Goddess of the Sky. Send down all your darkest power tonight so that we might work the special charm of the shade. Send your divine dark power to our fingertips.'

She nods at me and I repeat it sentence by sentence and when Selina lifts her arms and clasps her hands high above her head I do the same. I stare at the silver

174

moon and it seems to grow larger and larger, filling the room with its unearthly power, sending us spinning into its own strange orbit. I feel my fingers tingling, tingling with the power of the shade.

'We bless and sanctify these small instruments of evil in your shadowy name, Great Goddess,' says Selina, dropping her arms and sketching a crescent moon in the air above the box on the cushion. Then she takes a pin and holds it poised over the dough image. I lower my arms and watch, my hands tingling so badly I can hardly bear it.

# Chapter 22

We are sitting in the kitchen demurely nibbling jam tarts when Mrs Murray returns.

'How lovely to see you! Ah, a pot of tea. Pour me a cup, Selina darling.' She smiles at me. 'Did you bring the little cakes, dear?'

'I made them,' says Selina.

'My goodness, are you becoming domesticated at last?' says Mrs Murray, picking up a tart and taking a tentative bite. 'Mm. Not bad. For a first attempt. Although they're a bit underdone — and you've used far too much jam.'

'Actually it was May who made them, not me,' says Selina.

Mrs Murray raises her eyebrows and takes a long drink of tea. She's wearing a strange silvery lipstick that leaves an eerie smile on the rim of her cup.

'Selina's just teasing you, Mrs Murray.'

'I know, dear. I'm used to her funny little ways,' she says, tapping her long silver nails against the porcelain cup so that it tinkles. I watch, wondering if the nail varnish will rub off too. I imagine Mrs Murray lying down in her bed at night and a colourless spectre getting up in the morning, staring aghast at the new pattern on her sheet.

She's watching me too. I blush and look away. I know she's still looking at me. I take another jam tart for something to do, but the barely cooked dough is slippery in my mouth and the sweet slime of the red jam makes me choke.

'May doesn't appear to be appreciating your culinary efforts either,' says Mrs Murray. She yawns and stretches. 'I'm exhausted.' She edges closer to me. 'You'll never guess who I've been closeted with all afternoon.'

'Oh, Selina told me. Marie Holmwood. You were telling her fortune.'

'She told you, did she?' says Mrs Murray, her eyes flickering to meet Selina's. Then she relaxes. 'That's right, I do tell fortunes and I've built up a rather exclusive clientele. You'd be surprised if you knew who consults me. *Selina* would be surprised. She doesn't know everything — even if she thinks she does.'

'Do try a jam tart, Mother,' says Selina. 'It might choke you,' she adds under her breath.

'No thank you, darling. I suppose I'd better start preparing supper — unless Mrs Beeton here cares to take over altogether in the kitchen.'

'Oh no, Mother, I'm sure I'll never match your culinary expertise. Why, the expert way you switch on the microwave and shove in the Marks takeaways leaves me awestruck.'

Mrs Murray bares her teeth in a mock smile. Then she softens it for me.

'You're staying for supper, May?'

'Oh no thank you, Mrs Murray, I'd better be going. I didn't realise it was so late.' I try to finish my tea in one gulp. I'm used to tea bags at home and end up with a mouthful of tea-leaves.

'Spit them out, poppet,' says Mrs Murray, taking my cup and offering me her own Liberty print handkerchief. I swallow because it's too pretty to spoil. She's staring at the tea-leaves left in my cup.

'What is it?'

'Nothing, dear. Sorry. It's simply a matter of habit, reading the leaves.'

'Let me see. What has she got there?' Selina asks, coming over. She peers in the cup. 'Oh dear. A little serpent. Poor May.'

'What does a serpent mean?'

'I don't think it's a serpent,' says Mrs Murray, going to the sink, 'It's a lucky number seven. I'm sure it's a seven.'

She holds the cup under the tap and swills all the sevens and serpents down the plughole.

'Number seven is lucky?' I ask.

'The luckiest number of all. I was born on the 7th July, the seventh month of the year,' Mrs Murray declares. 'That's why I've been granted the gift of second sight. Although sometimes I wonder if it's more of a curse than a gift. I have sensed such terrible things in my time.'

'I've really got to go now,' I gabble and I back out of the kitchen.

Selina follows me to the door.

'Thanks for helping me, sister,' she whispers.

'I wish we hadn't done it. Oh Selina, can't you go upstairs and take all the pins out again?'

'Sh! She'll hear. Of course not. It's too late, anyway.'

'You mean something might have happened to Bruno already?'

'Shut *up*.'

'I wish you hadn't done it.'

'You did it too.'

'I didn't want to. Oh Selina, I'm scared.'

'I'd be scared if I had a serpent in my tea-leaves.'

'But it wasn't. Your mother said —'

'She was just trying to reassure you, stupid.'

'Well, what's so bad about a serpent anyway? I know what it means, so there. It means sex.'

'Oh, we've read a potted article on Freud, have we? Well, in the Craft terms it means much more. It's the symbol of Death and Corruption.'

I stare at her, speechless. She smiles but then she reaches out and takes hold of my arm.

'Hey stupid, it's not always. And it doesn't have to be your death. It could be a close relation. May, don't shake like that. I'm not positive it was a serpent. Maybe

178

it was a lucky number seven after all, like Mother said. May? May, come back.'

I can't. I've got to get home as quickly as I can. I've got to make sure Nan and Auntie Win are all right.

But they're there in the living room, safe if not sound. Auntie Win is frowning over a library book, Nan is holding her knitting, gently stroking the wool as if it is a pet.

'Hello,' I say, and I'm so relieved I want to put my arms around them and hug them both. 'I'm sorry about all that fuss before I went out.'

Nan smiles vaguely. Auntie Win sniffs.

'Shall I make tea?' I suggest, desperate to make friends with them again. 'What would you like? How about French toast, we haven't had that for ages.'

I remember too late that Grandad always used to put a piece of eggy toast on the end of his fork and make it talk Franglaise to amuse me.

'Your Grandad,' Nan begins, and Auntie Win looks up anxiously.

'I've got a nice smoked mackerel for each of us,' she says. 'And I've had the kettle boiled and the table laid this past half hour. Where have you been this time, young lady?'

'I'm not really late, you know I'm not. Auntie Win, please, don't get cross with me again. Shall I cut some bread and butter if we're having mackerel?'

'She's been out with her Grandad, I'll be bound,' says Nan, putting down her knitting and looking at me through her lop-sided glasses. 'Where did he take you this time, pet? Did you go and feed the ducks? I hope you haven't finished up all my bread!'

'Nan —'

'It was the swings! That's why you're looking as if you've got the collywobbles, he always pushes you too high, doesn't he? I'll have to have a word with him. Where is he, dearie? Changing his shoes? I hope he's not hiding in the bathroom having a naughty puff at his cigarette, he *knows* he ought to give it up. Where's your

179

Grandad, May?'

I shake my head helplessly and look at Auntie Win.

'Now don't start, Annie. Let's go and have tea now, eh? You like smoked mackerel, you're always saying how tasty it is.'

But when we've steered her into the kitchen for tea Nan gazes reproachfully at her plate.

'I thought you said it was French toast, May. That's a great favourite with your Grandad. Oh dear, this smoked mackerel. I'm sure it's very nice but he's never really cared for fish.'

Auntie Win tries to persuade her to eat it herself, but Nan will only prod it with a fork and eats one small mouthful. Auntie Win glares at me as if it's all my fault. I don't want to eat either. It's no use, I can't ever seem to do anything right now.

The metallic taste of the fish stays in my mouth all evening. Auntie Win gathers up the library book and knitting and switches on the television. Nan is nodding within minutes but her hands twitch and shake restlessly in her sleep as if she's counting phantom stitches. Auntie Win suggests I might do a little sketching. I don't want to draw anything ever again but I don't want another argument so I fetch a notebook and a pencil. I start to draw the spider plant on top of the television set. Each half of the plant spirals wildly on my paper and the pot starts to grow a face. The shading could be a pair of narrowed eyes. They're staring at me. It's not a plant in a pot, it's a terrifying woman with staring eyes, a Medusa with serpents sprouting from her scalp, serpents ...

I close the book with a snap and say I'm going to have an early night because I've got a headache. It's true, my whole head hurts, I feel as if someone's crammed a tight rubber bathing cap right over it. I crawl into bed and lie there rigidly, my arms folded across my chest. Like my image of Bruno. Oh let him be all right, *please.*

I don't know what to do. I did try to stop her but she

wouldn't listen. She never listens to me but I can't seem to help listening to her. I keep telling myself that those tea-leaves were in the shape of a lucky number seven but Selina's voice hisses sibilantly in my ears.

I try to make up a fairy tale with lots of lucky sevens in it. I think of all the fairy tales I've written down for Rob, the first one about the night, the ice story, the honey story, the two crones, the first child and the crow story, the crow child and the cruel princess, that makes six, so this seventh story should be about a seventh child.

Imagine, seven daughters in seven years! And six of the sisters were so beautiful, tall and slender, with golden curls. The seventh child was the runt of the litter. Small, stunted, white face and red hair, as ugly as can be. The six pretty sisters teased the littlest one, so that she stormed and shouted. Her father stormed and shouted too, telling her she was more trouble than all the others put together. Her father didn't love her. But her mother loved her. She said she loved her so much, why couldn't she be good and sweet and pretty like her sisters? Then the ugly child would feel so wretched she would creep out to the garden and cry.

She was weeping there one day when she saw a line of ants scurrying along the sandy path, little black wriggling ants. She stood where she was, wondering if they might wriggle right over her bare feet. But the ants advanced carefully along the edge of one foot, turned left above her toes and then came to a halt, so that they made a special shape. There was no mistaking it. It was a seven.

The next day she went into the garden for

another weep, and the ants came wriggling right up to her feet and formed the same shape. And the next day and the next. And the next day and the next after that. And on the seventh day they spoke.

'Do not weep, seventh sister. Wait seven more years — and then you will see what you will see.'

This cheered the Seventh Sister a little, although she felt she was in for rather a long wait. That year the eldest sister had her fourteenth birthday. She had grown so lovely that all the boys in the village clumped round to the cottage to woo her. The eldest sister smiled but shook her golden head. Then guess who came galloping by. Who else but a handsome prince. When he saw the eldest sister he was bewitched by her beauty. He beckoned her onto the back of his white steed and took her for a little ride. And then another little ride and another. And then one day they galloped off into the sunset, and perhaps they lived happily ever after.

The next year the second eldest sister had her fourteenth birthday, and she too had grown so lovely that all the boys in the village clumped round to the cottage to woo her. The second eldest sister smiled but shook her golden head (after dallying with several, just in case her prince might not come). But one day there was the sound of horses hooves outside the cottage and it was another handsome prince and when he saw the second eldest sister he was bewitched by her beauty. He didn't have to beckon for long. The second eldest sister jumped right up on to his horse and put her arms round his waist straight away. They galloped off into the sunset and maybe they lived happily ever after too.

182

And the next sister and the next. And the
next sister and quite possibly the next. But
what about the seventh sister, the littlest one,
the ugly runt?

She had her fourteenth birthday at long
last. She hadn't grown any lovelier. She had
stayed small and stunted, and her miserable
life gave her mouth a twist and her shoulders
a droop that did not increase her appeal. The
village boys clumped right past her without a
second glance. But time after time the ants in
the garden spelt out their special seven and
the seventh child did not lose heart. 'We will
see what we will see,' she whispered.

Sure enough, a handsome prince came
trotting up to the cottage on a milk white
steed. A really highborn handsome prince
with all the correct royal regalia. (Some of the
other princes had been rather suspect, very
flash in white satin shirts and red leather
buckled boots.) The seventh child was in the
garden, pulling up vegetables for supper. She
quickly threw the carrots to the ground and
rubbed her earthy hands on her apron. She
stared up at the handsome prince and just
for a second she really did seem to blossom.
Her eyes shone, her pale face flushed, her
brazen hair danced in the wind. The ants
spelt out their seven at her feet and muttered
'You will see what you will see.'

She saw the Prince. Her Prince. But he
was looking up at her window. And there
was her mother smiling at him as she
combed her long hair, still as gold as the sun.
The prince beckoned, bewitched. The
mother came down into the garden. She was
still lithe and lovely, even though she had
borne seven children. She smiled a little
uncertainly at her youngest child. She didn't

even waste a glance at her husband in his mud-caked hessian. She held up her arms to the Prince and he lifted her onto his white steed and they rode off into the sunset.

It was obvious they were never coming back. The husband stormed and shouted and then supped ale until he slumped in a stupour.

The Seventh Sister stayed in the garden and stamped on the ants.

# Chapter 23

Amy is laughing at me. She tosses her long golden hair and laughs and laughs, her blue eyes screwed into slits, her mouth wide open, her white even teeth glittering with saliva.

'May! May, wake up!'

I open my eyes and blink up at her in the sudden bright light. Her eyes blear, her colour pales, her skin wrinkles. I blink again and prop myself up on one elbow, staring at Auntie Win.

'What is it? Is it time to get up?'

'It's eleven o'clock, May, eleven o'clock, and I just don't know what to do.'

'Have I slept in?'

Perhaps I'm still sleeping now because nothing is making sense.

'It's eleven at *night*. You've only been in bed a couple of hours. Oh, *do* wake up, I need you to help me look for her.'

'For —?'

'For *Nan*! She's not here.'

I stare at Auntie Win.

'We were watching television — some silly chat show, I can't remember — your Nan was fast asleep, you know what she's like nowadays, and I kept trying to summon the energy to get her up the stairs to bed, but I was so tired myself, and so I must have dozed off — and then when I woke she wasn't there.'

'She'll be in the lavatory, Auntie Win.'

'Of course she's not!' Auntie Win snaps, making me jump. She struggles to control herself, nibbling at her thin lips with her large teeth. She nips at a bit of dry skin and pulls until it bleeds. 'Of course she's not in the lavatory,' she says, wiping the smears of blood with the back of her hand and keeping it pressed against her face. She speaks through it, and it makes her look so strange, as if she's gone mad, and I'm starting to feel scared of her, scared of this whole baffling nightmare.

'Then she'll be in the kitchen, filling her hot water bottle,' I suggest desperately.

'I've searched every single room in the house. I've even looked up in the loft. She's not out in the garden either, I've had a good look. So she must have gone out somewhere.'

'But she'd never go out, not at this time. You know she wouldn't. She's terrified of getting mugged. And where would she go? She never goes out, and she'd never in a million years go out this late.'

'Then where is she? She can't have vanished into thin air.'

'She'll be in the house,' I insist, and I leap out of bed and start running crazily from room to room, calling Nan's name. I search her own bedroom from top to bottom, pulling down the bedclothes, even peering underneath. I open her wardrobe and go through all the clothes. Grandad's suits are still there, and the faint smell of him makes my eyes sting. I rest for a second, holding his jacket sleeve up to my face, sniffling because his arms can never be inside it, and then my sorrow tips over into panic on Nan's behalf.

'She's dead! Oh no, what if she's dead!'

'Stop that! Of course she isn't. She's just wandered off. We'll have to phone the police, get them to look for her,' says Auntie Win. 'Come on, May, there's no point looking, she can't possibly be in the house. There now, stop that silly crying, we'll soon find her. I'm sorry, maybe I shouldn't have woken you. It was just such a shock waking up myself and seeing her chair empty, her

186

knitting all over the floor, and not another trace of her in the house. Look, I'll put my coat on and run down to the end of the road just in case she's anywhere nearby, and then if there's no sign of her I'll ring the police. You put the kettle on for me, dear. I won't be five minutes, all right? And don't answer the door unless it's my special knock, do you hear me?'

I don't want her to go. I'm so scared of being left by myself in the house, scared that she won't come back either and I'll be left alone for ever. But I'm not a baby, I can't very well cling to her, so I let her go and wait downstairs in the kitchen.

The kettle starts to hiss. And my thoughts hiss inside my head. First Grandad. And now Nan. I start shivering violently and clasp my hands. I wonder if I should try to pray. I don't know any prayers, only the Lord's Prayer, but I can't remember all the words, so I gabble Our Father Our Father over and over again. Only I haven't got a father, I haven't got a mother either, although she's up there in my room, smiling for ever in black and white, white and black, the light and the shade, I want so badly to get away from the shade, so I close my eyes and try to think of white but the world behind my lids is black, and though I think of fields of snow, forests of frost, a pure white land where the sun never sets the black obliterates it at a blink. I put my hands over my eyes and stare right down into the darkness, trying to see what is at the very bottom, wondering how far I still have to tumble — and then I hear a key in the door, shuffling footsteps, voices —

Nan's voice, mildly surprised: 'I just popped out to look, dear. I just popped out. I just popped out to look for May.'

I run into the hall. Nan is standing shaking her head in meek bewilderment. She seems to be wearing a gigantic padded coat that trails on the ground. Auntie Win is supporting her at one side — and astonishingly, Mrs Roberts is at the other.

'Nan! Were you looking for me? Here I am. I've been

187

in all evening, don't you remember, and I went up to bed early because I didn't feel well. I was upstairs in bed, Nan.'

She blinks at me.

'Then why did your Grandad go out looking for you, dear?'

I'm silenced. I glance at Mrs Roberts. Her eyes are gleaming.

'Don't you try explaining to Nannie just now, pet, she's a bit mixed up,' says Mrs Roberts, pulling at Nan's arms. 'Come on, Win, let's get her to bed. Best thing all round. She's still as cold as ice although I gave her a nice hot cuppa and wrapped my spare room duvet round her. My God, my heart's still pounding. It gave me such a turn when I went to put the milk bottles out. There she was, right by my garden gate, calling for you-know-who so pathetically —'

'Yes, well, it was very kind of you to take her in, but you really should have phoned me straight away,' says Auntie Win. She is trying to unravel Nan from Mrs Roberts' duvet.

'Oh no, dear, leave that on her.' She raises her voice as if Nan is deaf. 'Come on, my lovie, up the little wooden stairs to Bedfordshire.'

'I'll manage now. Thank you for all your trouble. And here, you must have this back.' Auntie Win wrenches it from Nan and then sees the dark stain inside it. She blushes.

'Never mind, never mind, these little accidents will happen when they get to that age,' says Mrs Roberts. 'I'm sure it'll wash in a tick. And it's only the spare room duvet, so even if the stain doesn't come out it's not really —'

'We'll get you another,' says Auntie Win weakly.

My own face is burning. I'd give anything to be up in my room, under my bedclothes, away from this awfulness.

'May!' Auntie Win calls me. 'May, come and give me a hand with Nan. Thank you so much for your help,

188

Mrs Roberts. We must let you get home now.'

'Don't be like that, dear. You let young May get back to bed. She looks a bit upset. It's not very nice for her to see her Nannie in a bit of a pickle, I know. But I'm used to it, dear, don't worry. I nursed my own mother right up until the end. I know what they can be like. So I'll give you a hand bathing her and then we'll get her into bed.' She raises her voice again. 'That's what you'd like, lovie, isn't it? Nice hot bath to clean you up a bit and then comfy old bed. Have you get an electric blanket, eh? Oh well, a nice hot water bottle instead.'

Auntie Win looks as if she's been scalded by all this nice hot water. She argues, but Mrs Roberts has Nan by the arm and is already hustling her upstairs. I reboil the kettle, fill the hot pig, and wrap it in its old vest. It is one of Nan's old vests, salmon pink and very soft, but it's grubby now and I hate the thought of Mrs Roberts seeing it. I wonder about using one of Nan's good vests, she's got three, one on, one in the drawer and one in the wash, but nowadays they all seem to be in the wash. I open the drawer of Grandad's underwear instead and finger his limp white garments, but it's like touching his own limp white flesh and I shut the drawer up quickly.

I go to my own room, hoping to hide there until Nan's in bed and Mrs Roberts has departed, but I can't escape, Auntie Win calls for me to find Nan's clean nightie in the special quilted nightdress case. Nan's clean nightie is in the airing cupboard, as Auntie Win and I well know; the nightdress in the quilted case has never been worn. It is Nan's just-in-case-of-hospital nightie. And Nan knows this very well too and starts fussing when Auntie Win slips it over her head.

'You're sending me away, I know it. You're putting me in a home. You're getting me ready for the ambulance!'

Auntie Win does her best to reassure her but she can hardly explain about impressing Mrs Roberts when Mrs Roberts herself is trying to soothe Nan too, cooing at her in an idiotic manner as if Nan is a naughty toddler:

'Come on, lovie, of course we're not sending you away. Let's get some bedsocks on those cold tootsies, there's a good girl, and what's all this fuss about your nightie, it's a very pretty nightie.'

Nan cowers away from her, clutching at Auntie Win.

'Don't send me away, Win, for pity's sake,' she begs. 'I know I get a bit muddled and I can't always manage, but I'll try harder, I swear I will. Win, please. I've been good to you in the past, haven't I? I've put up with a great deal, more than most, I've —'

'Oh do shut up, Annie,' Auntie Win shouts, shaking her. 'Do try and get a grip on yourself. Of course you're not being sent away. You're here in your own house, all right, and that's where you're going to stay. So stop making all this fuss and let's get you into bed.'

But Nan doesn't seem to hear her. She plucks at the smooth nylon of her nightdress in her distress.

'I never turned you away, Win, even when —'

'Stop it! Now stop making an exhibition of yourself and get into bed!' Auntie Win shouts, shaking her harder, making her stagger.

'Hey, hey, gently does it,' says Mrs Roberts, steadying Nan, and giving Auntie Win a little pat on the shoulder. 'I know, dearie, they do get you down at times, and it's a strain when you're not a young woman yourself, but it doesn't help to lose your temper. Look now, you've upset her, poor dear.' She cuddles in to Nan. 'There now, lovie, Sis didn't mean it, don't take on.'

'I think we'd be better off if we were left on our own,' says Auntie Win, struggling so hard to stay in control that she says each word very slowly, like a Dalek. 'May, show Mrs Roberts out, will you? Thank you again for all your help, it's so kind of you.'

'Now then, Win, no need to get on your high horse. We're all girls together, aren't we? I know it's a strain, but I don't mind coming round and sitting with the old lady once in a while to give you a break. We always got on so well in the past, Annie and Arthur and me.'

'Where's Arthur got to?' Nan sobs. 'I've looked and looked and it's bad for him to be out this late, he's got a dicky heart.'

'Don't you worry about Arthur, dear. He's happy where he is and you'll meet up with him in due course,' says Mrs Roberts with sentimental authority.

'He's been such a good husband to me, in spite of everything. Of course, I had my cross to bear, but I could never think of leaving Arthur, never, oh no —'

'Come on, Annie, *bed.*'

'You shouldn't keep trying to take her mind off him, dear. You should let her ramble on, cry it all out. It might do her the power of good, stop her going so funny in the head, if you want my opinion.'

'I don't want your opinion. I'm sick to death of hearing your opinion. So will you please get out of this house, you interfering busybody,' Auntie Win yells at the top of her voice.

We are all shocked into silence. Mrs Roberts pulls her coat round herself, her face pinched.

'Thank you very much, I'm sure,' she says. 'You shouldn't use that tone of voice with me, Your Ladyship. You might be very sorry you've treated me like dirt, when I've done my best to be a good friend and neighbour.'

She kicks the soiled duvet out of her way and goes downstairs. I'm scared she'll start spreading it round the whole street that Nan ruined her wretched duvet and so I run after her, although Auntie Win keeps calling me back.

I catch Mrs Roberts at the front door.

'I'm sorry, Mrs Roberts, Auntie Win didn't mean to be so rude. She's just worried about Nan, that's all.'

'Worried what she'll say next,' says Mrs Roberts. 'The nerve she's got. There's me rolling up my sleeves, bathing the old lady, doing all the dirty bits because your precious Auntie Win just stood there, dithering and dabbing uselessly —'

She goes on and on, and I know she'll tell all her

191

friends, all the neighbours, and they'll tell it too. I see why we've always kept to ourselves, I see why Auntie Win detests Mrs Roberts. She *is* a busybody, her whole body is busy with our business, head waggling, eyebrows wiggling, breasts wobbling.

'You're the one I feel sorry for, young May,' she says, and she clucks at me like a chicken.

'I'm all right.'

'You poor little scrap.'

'I'm all *right*. I'm fine. I think you ought to go now.'

'Oh, my, now I'm getting my marching orders from a little madam like you. Hoity toity.' She jerks her shoulders as she repeats it, turning herself into a pantomime.

'No wonder Auntie Win was rude to you.'

Her face stops moving. It sets into stone.

'Why do you call her Auntie, eh?' she hisses. 'She's not your Auntie.'

'I know. She's my great aunt.'

'Oh no, she's not. Well, half the folks round here don't think she is anyway.' She pokes her head forward until it's only an inch from mine. 'We think *she's* your Nan.'

The words don't make sense. How can Auntie Win be Nan? And then I see the leer in her face and I understand. She walks away and I shut the door on her. I stand still.

I try to say the words in my head. Grandad and Nan and Auntie Win and Amy. I imagine them like dolls in front of me. I take Nan away from Grandad. I put Auntie Win beside him instead. Then I stand her in the corner and give her baby Amy. Then Nan comes and takes the baby and stands beside Grandad again. And Auntie Win is allowed out of her corner, although she never gets to stand beside Grandad again. And then the Amy doll gets bigger and bigger and there's suddenly a new baby doll. Amy gets smashed to pieces. And Nan comes and takes this new baby. Me.

It can't be true. It's just spiteful gossip. Auntie Win's never been to bed with anyone in her life, she's just not

192

the sort — and as if she'd ever do it with *Grandad.* And then how could they live together afterwards, from corn-flakes at breakfast till cocoa at bedtime, day after day, with never a cross word, no shouting, no screaming, no sobbing.

Until now.

'May! Has she gone? What are you doing down there? Come up to bed, for goodness sake. I've got Nan settled at last.'

I walk very slowly up the stairs. I want to settle myself. I want to know. I want to tell Auntie Win what Mrs Roberts said and watch her face, and then I'll know if there's any truth in it.

And yet when I just think the words in my head I go hot, so hot I feel as if I'm on fire. I face Auntie Win but I'm burning all over.

'What's up with you?'

I shake my head.

'Don't take it to heart so. It's all over now. You go to bed. I'd better put this wretched duvet to soak.'

'Auntie Win, Mrs Roberts said —'

I'm stuck. I can't say it.

'Never mind about that dreadful woman, she's gone now.' Auntie Win ducks her head. 'I don't know what came over me, shouting at her like that.'

'I'm glad you did.'

'No, it was very silly and rude.' Auntie Win folds up the duvet and holds it well away from her. Then she meets my eye. 'But I'm glad I did too,' she says, and she smiles at me.

It's only a twinkle and then her face goes tense again. Is it anything like Amy's smile? Is she Amy's mother? My grandmother?

I try to whisper the words when she's downstairs in the kitchen, but my lips stay shut, sealing them inside.

# Chapter 24

'Selina!' I catch her outside the cloakroom. 'Is he all right? Have you heard anything?'

Selina looks at me blankly.

'Bruno! Has it worked?'

'What are you on about, May?' she says, fiddling with her hair. 'Look, do you think it would suit me if I had it over to one side like this?'

'Selina, please, stop playing games. Have you seen Bruno?'

'Of course not,' Selina says coldly.

'Bruno? Is that the gorgeous blond hunk, ever so trendy?' Louise asks, squeezing past us. 'Are you still going with him?'

'Him!' says Selina. 'No fear. I can't stick him now.'

'Oh yeah?' says Louise, and there's a little smirk on her face.

Selina stalks off down the corridor. I run after her.

'Selina, do you think he's all right?'

'How the hell should I know?'

'Don't you think you ought to get in touch?'

'Don't you think you ought to shut your stupid face?'

'Selina, don't. I'm sorry Louise heard. I didn't realise she was there.'

'As if I care about her. Or you, for that matter.'

'You still care about Bruno.'

'I'm not the faintest bit interested in boring old Bruno.'

'So why did you bother to do all that black magic stuff on Saturday?'

'Black magic! You are ridiculous.'

'No, you're the one who's ridiculous. I never know where I am with you. You just keep messing me about. You're sick.'

'You're the one who's sick, little precious. Watch out I don't make you even sicker. I could take my pins and go prick prick prick.' She flicks at me with her long fingernails, hurting me.

I stand still, trying not to cry. She smiles at me and brushes past. I can't face the thought of going into the classroom after her. I blunder down the corridor, oh no, *no.*

'Hello May. How are you?'

'All right,' I mumble, not looking at him.

'Thanks very much for the shortbread. It was lovely.'

'That's okay.'

I try to walk past but he hangs on to my sleeve.

'You'd better watch out. Someone might see.'

'Don't, May. Please. I didn't mean ... Can't we be friends?'

I won't answer. But I go to his lesson. He reads *The Little Mermaid* to us today. I know the story and yet now the details make me sit up straight. I prickle as if oysters are clamped to my own skin. The little mermaid is an odd withdrawn child who plays by herself. She is allowed to rise to the surface of the sea on her fifteenth birthday. She falls so passionately in love with the handsome prince that she consults the terrifying sea witch, willing to try the most desperate black charm to obtain the legs that will let her walk above the water and dance to his desire.

Rob reads the story well. Kath and her cronies groan and mutter through the first few paragraphs but they are soon still, their eyes on Rob as they listen. But he's not telling the story for them. He's telling it to me. It's his secret message to me, I know it is. He's wearing his black sweater and I stare at the red heart and I know that he is mine after all. But it's no use waiting. I am the one with the black charm. The prince knows he can't dive down into the deep water because he will

195

drown. But the little mermaid can stand on her own two feet.

'Do you want to come round to my place?' Selina says to me after school, as if this morning's row had never happened.

'No thanks.'

'Why? Oh God, are you still scared of what Auntie Whatsit and Ninny-Nanny might say?'

'No. I don't want to come because I don't want to be friends with you any more,' I say, and I push past.

I am diving right down into the ocean, away from everyone, swimming until I have the strength to surface, and now I'm at Rob's street and I'm coming up into the air now, my lungs are hurting with the shock, but my steps don't falter even though every pace means pain.

I ring his bell but he's not back yet. The glass on the front door is still broken, so I slip my hand through carefully and open it up for myself. The smell in the hall is overpowering. Perhaps the old lady in the downstairs flat has fallen, perhaps she's been lying there for weeks, silently rotting, whilst the squatters squat above her and Rob writes in his attic rooms above them. I stare at the door of the downstairs flat. Perhaps she's lying just the other side of it, her stiffened hand forever reaching for the handle . . . It turns, the door opens, and the old lady hobbles out, tap shuffle shuffle, tap shuffle shuffle, first her walking frame and then her feet in their old check slippers.

'What's up with you?' she demands.

'Nothing, I—'

'Why are you hanging around downstairs, eh? You get up to the floor where you belong. Although you won't be there much longer, you wait and see. I've written to the council about you.'

She thinks I'm one of the squatters. I run upstairs, past the two flats they've taken over, and up to Rob's attic. Perhaps I'll become a real squatter. What if I set up home here on the stairs? Or inside, with Rob. I'm small, I wouldn't take up much room, and I'm quiet,

I'd let him get on with his writing in peace. I wouldn't go to school. I'd read and write and paint all day, and I'd clean up the room and I'd cover up all the hot clashing colour, I'd paint a night of navy blue and indigo, and I'd make a dark quilt sprinkled with stars and a silver moon and we'd slide under our own midnight sky and sleep together.

We will sleep together. We will make love. I don't care if it's wrong. And how can Nan and Auntie Win dare say it's wrong when they both slept with the same man? Well, they might have done. And anyway, even if Mrs Roberts was telling a lot of lies, then Selina's done it, she's done it with Bruno and probably with lots of other boys too, and yet I know she's never loved any of them the way I love Rob. I love him, I love him, I love him, I love him, I love him, I love him, I love him —

'May?'

'Oh!'

'What are you doing here?'

He doesn't look pleased to see me.

'I thought I'd —'

'Look, I thought we agreed it might be more sensible if you didn't come round. Well, not like this, by yourself.'

'You want me to bring someone with me?'

'No. You know what I mean.'

'I'm sorry. I just — after that story you read — I wanted to talk about it.'

'But I asked you what you thought of it in class and you just shrugged and wouldn't say anything. I was relying on you to help me out. None of the others seemed to have much to say, did they, just the usual "Bit boring" and "Babyish" and "Oh Mr Campbell why do you always go on about symbols" and "If you ask me these feminists are just a bunch of Lessies so who cares what they think?"'

I can't smile. My eyes are stinging. I hate him being cross with me. Perhaps he wasn't sending me a message after all. Perhaps he's sick of me. Perhaps he thinks I'm a silly little baby too.

'I'm sorry. I'll go.'

'Oh come on. You're here now. Come in and have a cup of tea. I haven't got any doughnuts today but I can rustle up a jam sandwich.'

'It's all right. I'm not hungry. Are you very cross with me?' I ask, as I go into his flat and sit on the cold leatherette chair. The midnight blue in my mind was so real that the harsh colour startles me. There's no magic quilt on his studio couch, only ugly lemon candlewick.

'Of course I'm not really cross with you, dopey,' says Rob, filling the kettle.

He makes tea for us, talking about school, telling me about the First Years' reaction to *The Little Mermaid*, and how one little girl has written her own modern version with the sea all polluted with oil and the handsome prince turned into the captain of a Polaris submarine. I don't think it's such an original idea and I don't see why he's so impressed by this boring little twelve year old. And then he asks me what I think of the story, but how can I tell him when the kettle's whistling and he's in the middle of making jam sandwiches? I clutch the arms of the leatherette chair and try to start, but I can't find any of the right words. I shrug and stammer just the way I did in class. I know it would be all right if he'd only stop making those stupid sandwiches, if he'd only come and sit on the arm of the chair beside me, if he'd only hold me close so that I could whisper what I want. Like this I'm as dumb as the little mermaid herself.

'I thought you wanted to talk about *The Little Mermaid*?' says Rob. 'Oh hell. I've run out of teabags.'

'It doesn't matter, really. I don't want tea. About *The Little Mermaid*. You see, I don't know whether you really meant me to think this, but I couldn't help feeling she was like me.'

'Of course. Hans Anderson is the champion of the sensitive, the sad, everyone who's ever felt an odd one out. Think of *The Ugly Duckling*, *The Steadfast Tin*

198

*Soldier, The Little Match Girl.* But I think *The Little Mermaid* is the most powerful of all — and it's so touching because it's a doomed love right from the start. We know it couldn't possibly have a happy ending. Coffee then? Although I've only got some cheap supermarket stuff that's suspiciously like gravy browning.'

'I don't want anything, really. *The Little Mermaid* could have a happy ending. I mean the Prince could realise in time, and fall in love with her and not bother with that other girl.'

'But that's the point, May. *I'd* like tea. I'll dash down and see if Miss Murdoch's got any she'll lend me. I carried her shopping bag home from the parade the other day so she thinks I'm Prince Charming at the moment.'

'That's what the girls in our class call you. Prince Charming.'

'Do they? Cheeky little things!' Rob sounds enchanted with the idea.

I let go the chair when he's gone. There are moist smears on the leatherette because I've been clutching it so hard. Its no use. He didn't mean me to come here. I don't think he really does love me. He's just as keen on that stupid first year, or the girls in my class. I'm wasting my time. I might as well go home.

I stand up and wander round his room, fingering the shabby furniture, flicking through a book, fidgetting with a pile of papers on the table. It's manuscript. His new novel? I glance at the door cautiously, wondering how long it will take him to get downstairs and back. Miss Murdoch will probably be ages fumbling with tea caddies. And I'll hear his footsteps anyway.

I shouldn't read it. I know it's private. And yet I'll be able to read it when it's published, won't I?

"I don't know what I'm going to do. I love her so much and yet I hardly dare look at her when we're in school. She was standing two rows in front of me in Assembly, so small and sweet and serious, and the sun was shining through the window onto her long

199

marigold plait, and I ached to untie it and let it loose all around her like a mandala in a medieval painting, I wanted to kneel down and worship her —"

My hands are shaking so badly I can hardly keep the paper still. He does love me. He does. Only he's as scared as I am, and that's why he's going on about *The Little Mermaid* and making such a thing about the tea and coffee now — because he's scared. He'll never dare make a move, so it's going to have to be me.

I put the paper back and stand still. I close my eyes and look up, imagining the great silver globe in the night sky. I raise my arms.

'Oh Great Goddess, help me. I don't know what to do and I'm scared it might hurt or I might make a fool of myself. So please help me. Let me bewitch him so that he is mine for ever.'

I lower my arms and then start tugging at my hair, unfastening my plait and combing it quickly with my fingers. I think those are his footsteps. I run to his bed and lie down on it, spreading my hair out decoratively. My fingers get tangled, I can't get my skirt straight, and my heart is swelling alarmingly, a great beach ball thudding up and down inside my chest. He's coming, he's coming, oh Great Goddess, help me.

'May?'

I daren't look at him. My eyes are closed. A little pulse beats in my eyelids as I wait. He waits too. Then I hear him come nearer.

'May, are you all right?'

I open my eyes and he's bending over me, nearer than I thought, his head very close to mine. I look into his eyes and then I smile. I know how to do it, I've stared at that smile every day of my life.

'Of course I'm all right,' I whisper, and then I wind my arms round his neck and pull him even closer. He's not expecting it and his mouth is open, so that his teeth bump against my lip, hurting me a little. But I press my lips properly against his, wondering whether I ought to open my mouth too, waiting to feel his body on mine.

200

But he's not kissing me, he's struggling, untangling my arms, pushing me away, pushing me —

'Stop it. May, for God's sake, what are you playing at? *Stop* it.'

'I only — I want — Please —'

'Sit up. And stop this nonsense.' His voice is harsh and hateful. I look at him and then I start burning. The fire flames in my face, my neck, right down my arms. I start crying, but even my tears are hot.

'Oh come on. Don't cry. It's all right. I don't know how you could have thought — May, do stop snivelling and pull yourself together. Here, sit up.'

He tries to pull me up, quite gently, but I swivel away from him, hunched into a ball. My eyes are tightly shut but the tears squeeze out from under my lids.

'There now. Look. There's no need to act like it's the end of the world. It was just a mad little impulse. I know, you've been through a lot recently, you're all mixed up, you probably didn't quite realise what you were doing.'

'Yes I did,' I sob. 'Don't pretend. I love you. And you love me.'

He sighs and tries to touch my shoulder, but I pull away from him. 'May, you don't love me. Not in that sort of way. You're just missing your Grandfather and —'

'You're talking rubbish,' I shout, sitting up and wiping my eyes on his bedspread. It smells sour and I fling it away from me. 'I love you properly. And you love me, I know you do.'

'May, I like you, I'm fond of you, you remind me a little bit of my own daughter —'

'That's lies, you hypocrite. I've seen what you've written, I've read it.'

'What?' He glances at the manuscript on the table. 'You had no business reading that.' He's really angry now. 'But it's not about you — or me. It's my novel, May, my new book about Mark. He's in love with this girl in the year below him at school —'

201

'It's me. She's got long red hair in a plait. No-one else has hair like that now.'

'All right, I've used your hair. I think you've got lovely hair and I borrowed it for my book, but that's all. The girl in my book, she's not a bit like you, apart from her hair, she's a different sort of girl altogether. It's a work of fiction, a story.'

'You go on and on about the hidden meanings in stories.'

'All right, I know that, but you're reading all sorts of meanings that were never ever meant.'

'Then why did you ever get talking to me? Why did you ask me round here in the first place?'

'I know, I shouldn't have done that.'

'And you held my hand the last time I was here.'

'It was just a game.'

'You're playing games now. You just twist things whichever way you want.'

'No I don't. It's you who gets things mixed up. Now calm down, let's both have this cup of tea and —'

'I don't want your rotten tea. I don't want anything from you ever again. You're just a hateful coward, a hateful hypocritical coward.'

'Stop shouting.'

'I won't, I won't. You're just scared someone will hear and think you're raping me or something.'

'You're being really childish now.'

'I'm sick to death of people calling me childish. I'm not a baby and you know it. That's why you won't kiss me. You don't dare because you want to so much.'

'I don't want you, May. That's the point,' he says, and he's calm now, and oh so cold. 'Don't you understand? You're just a sad little girl and I feel sorry for you.'

The fire flames. It's burning me right up. I know I'll never feel whole again. I stumble to my feet and run out of the room. He calls after me but I'm not listening. I don't love him. I hate him. I hate him I hate him I hate him.

202

# Chapter 25

At long long last I hear Auntie Win shuffle along the landing to the bathroom. A minute later she creeps downstairs, her backless slippers softly flapping at each step. She's in the kitchen, stoking the boiler, and then the water rushes as she fills the kettle. I wait and she waits too downstairs. I picture her sitting there, pleating the quilts of her pale pink dressing gown, flexing her long fingers, yawning. Then the kettle boils and she makes tea, a quick teabag in each cup, we don't bother with proper pots and paraphernalia now that Grandad's not here. And up the stairs, clink and flap, a little sigh when she gets to the top, and then it's into Nan's room and back to her own. She doesn't deliver a cup to me. I've told her I don't want early morning tea any more. It has got earlier and earlier since Grandad died.

I lie here, waiting. I have waited all night long. I haven't slept. I haven't even closed my eyes. They are burning now. I remember my story about the girl in the woods who had to stitch her eyes open. That was for love of the man in the night. I don't love any more. I hate. I hate. I am hot with hate as I toss in my tumbled bed.

I wait and wait for Auntie Win to get up again. These last ten minutes seem longer than the whole of the long biack night. I keep hearing phantom creaks of her bed, flaps of her slippers, but then nothing happens and I'm forced to wait on, watching the hands on Amy's little clock edge round each Roman numeral until the creak and flap is unmistakable. I hear the bathroom door close and the sudden roar of both taps and I leap out of bed.

Auntie Win has first turn in the bathroom now and she makes the most of it. She lies in her lavender bath salts, setting her hair in the steam. She won't hear me in there. And I don't need to worry about Nan. Two sips of her tea and then she's snoring again.

I run downstairs, rolling up the sleeves of my night-dress. I shut the kitchen door behind me and turn on the oven as high as it will go. Then I find the mixing bowl and a packet of flour. I won't need any fat, any milk. I want my mixture to be stark and sour. I add a little lemon juice until the dough is stiff enough to model. I stop and stare up at the ceiling. I stare right through my own empty bedroom, through the roof to the sky above and the silver moon. I raise my arms and I pray to the Goddess.

'Do not fail me now, Great Goddess. I do not want the power of the light. I want the power of the shade. The power of the shade. The power of the shade.'

I mutter it again and again as I lower my tingling hands and plunge them in the sticky dough. I fashion a head, a body, two arms, two legs. A small shape of a man, clumsy and a little lop-sided, but there's no time to make it perfect. I stretch him out on a greased tray and put him to bake in the top of the oven. Then I sit, watching the oven door, imagining the little dough man inside stretched out on the tray as if he's sunbathing.

I can't wait until he's properly tanned in case Auntie Win's beauty routine is curtailed for any reason. I switch off the oven and remove him when he's still pale and pasty. I used plain flour so he's still slim. Oh he keeps his figure well, he likes to trot about in his tight jeans.

I need pins but I don't have any, and the sewing box is in Auntie Win's bedroom. There's a packet of nails in the kitchen drawer, they'll have to do. Little black nails for pinning things on the kitchen wall: the kitten calendar, the Mabel Lucy Attwell motto, my old drawings and paintings. Auntie Win pinned up the careful pencil drawing of the seashells, the one that he scorned. Well, he won't scorn me any more. I'll show him. The power of the shade is tingling in my fingertips. I take a nail and pierce the little pastry man's chest. The hot dough gives a little sigh as I prick it — and suddenly it's not a lump of flour and juice, it's real flesh and blood, and the little black nail is a dagger and it's plunged up to its hilt in his heart, the red heart-shaped motif on his sweater, only now it's getting redder and redder, his black sweater is reddening with blood, it's Rob lying there and it's my hand on the knife and oh God what am I doing, what's that noise, the terrible noise, that scream, I'm screaming.

I pull out the nail and rub frantically at the dough to erase the little hole, and then I batten my hands over my mouth to try to stop the screams.

'May? May, whatever is it? Have you hurt yourself?' Auntie Win shouts from the bathroom, and Nan has started too, crying my name again and again like a plaintive bird.

'I'm all right. I just — I just — I'm okay, honestly.'

'I'll be down in a minute,' Auntie Win calls anxiously. 'Annie, it's all right, stop that calling, she's all right.'

I am not all right. I am all wrong. I look at the dough and the nails and my own shaking hands. I can't believe what I've done. And to Rob. Of course I don't hate him. I don't want to hurt him, how could I have ever wanted to hurt him? I hear the bathroom door slam. She'll be down any minute. What shall I do? Where can I hide the dough? I seize the shape, rush to the boiler, open the lid and drop it down onto the coals. The flames lick it and the limbs blacken as he burns. He is burning.

'No! No, I didn't mean it!' I cry, and I try to snatch him back but the coal is red hot and I can't save him. I drop the lid and stand wringing my hands and crying.

'Whatever are you up to?' says Auntie Win, bursting

205

into the kitchen. Her face is red from her bath, her rollers are hanging from her hair and her frock is unbuttoned.

'I–I've burnt my hand,' I sob.

'What do you mean? Let me see. Oh dear, oh dear, under the cold water tap, that'll take the sting out.'

'It's butter for burns, there's a half pound of Anchor in the fridge,' says Nan, coming into the kitchen with Grandpa's old check dressing gown pulled on over her nightie. 'Oh poor pet! Does it really hurt? Poor old tuppenny.' She pats at me while Auntie Win sticks my hand under the cold tap. There's a faint scent of Grandad still clinging to the grubby woollen dressing gown and it makes me cry more.

'Come on now. It's not that big a burn. Don't be such a baby,' says Auntie Win. 'And watch what you're doing, you're splashing water all over me. Here, let's have a look at it.' She turns off the tap and inspects my hand.

'You'll live,' she says, dabbing it dry with the tea-towel.

'Now the butter, Win.'

'Oh don't be silly, Annie, she's much better off with Savlon. In the kitchen drawer. Why have you been at it, May? What have you got those nails for? What have you been *up* to?'

'I was look for — for the wooden spoon. I wanted to do some baking. I wanted to make some bread rolls for breakfast but they went wrong.'

'Is that what the smell is? They're burning, you ninny,' says Auntie Win, opening the oven and peering inside.

'I threw them in the boiler because they didn't work.'

'You silly girl, you shouldn't do that. You'll set the whole kitchen ablaze if you're not careful. So that's how you got burnt.'

'Did you say you've made rolls, dearie? They'll make a nice change for breakfast,' says Nan politely, fetching the butter although Auntie Win is busy rubbing Savlon onto the red mark on my hand.

'They went wrong, Nan,' I sob. 'It all went wrong.'

'Well of course it went wrong,' says Auntie Win. 'You didn't know what you were doing. What ingredients did you use, for Heaven's sake? You can't have used any yeast because I haven't got any. How can you make bread rolls without yeast, you silly girl?'

'Don't carry on at her, Win. She meant well, didn't you, dear?' says Nan.

I didn't mean well. I meant harm. It's all gone wrong. I don't know what to do. I love him, I don't hate him, I don't want to harm him. I'll go and find him at school today. I'll try and tell him. I'll say I'm sorry about yesterday, I'll do anything, just so long as he's still all right and I haven't hurt him. I've got to try to make everything all right. By the power of the light. The power of the light. The power —

'What are you muttering?' says Auntie Win. 'Here May, you get the kettle on and the table laid while I go and finish in the bathroom. And Annie, you'd better get your proper clothes on, you shouldn't wander round in that dressing gown. It's much too long, you'll trip before you know where you are.'

'Don't say that! Don't tempt fate.'

'Oh don't be so silly, May. You never used to be so superstitious. I don't know what's the matter with you recently. You've never had much common sense but now you're acting plain daft — and so disobedient with it. What's got into you, eh?'

I can't tell her. I can't explain it even to myself. She's right though, there is something inside me now. I can feel it sizzle and stir and spit, and I can't seem to stop it. The boiler still smells of burning. It's making me feel sick. I open the kitchen window and try to waft in some fresh air but the burning smell won't go away.

I hear a fire engine go by outside. And then another. The sirens go on screaming in my ears. They were going up towards the old part of the town. To a fire. A fire. A fire.

I grab Auntie Win's gardening jacket from the back door and start running. My nightdress billows past my knees, my feet are bare on the cold hard pavement but I pound along as quickly as I can. The milkman stops and stares at me, a woman calls after me, two boys on bikes burst out laughing, but they blur into the background. The fire sirens go on shrieking in my head, and I can't hear, I can't see, I can't breathe, but I've got to go on running and running and running, I've got to get to him in time. I know he's burning, I know it's all my fault, I know it's the power of the shade, and I didn't know what I was doing, and now it's too late, oh don't let it be too late, let me be in time, help me, let me, let him be.

I turn into his street and there they are, both red engines, I knew it, I knew it was his house, I knew it was my spell, I couldn't stop the power of the shade, the fire is in me, it's tingling in my fingertips, crackling in my long red hair, burning in my face and now Rob is burning too, blackening in the manifestation of my own hell fire.

'Rob! Rob! Rob!' I scream although I've got no voice left.

I race towards the house. There's a crowd gathered round it. Someone tries to stop me, someone hangs on to me, but I scream and struggle and then suddenly Rob is there, the real Rob in his black sweater, and I fling myself at him and he holds me tight and I sob against him, unable to believe he's really safe.

'I was so sure you'd burn to death and it would be all my fault,' I gasp, clinging to him. 'I saw you burning in the fire and it was so terrible.'

'What fire? There isn't a fire,' says Rob, speaking slowly, trying to soothe me.

'This fire. I knew when I heard the sirens —'

'There's no fire. It was an explosion. Poor old Miss Murdoch's gas stove. She went to light it to boil her kettle and it blew up in her face. It lifted her right to the other side of the room, but they don't think she's broken anything. Her room's a wreck, of course, and

208

the whole house reeks of gas — the gas men are working on it now, they say there's been a leak for ages, that's why there's been that awful smell.'

I shake my head frantically.

'It was me, it was *me*.'

'What do you mean, love?' says one of the firemen.

'She's just hysterical,' says Rob.

'Is she one of the squatters? We were wondering if they'd been monkeying around with the gas.'

'No, she doesn't live here at all, she's —' Rob holds me away from him, looking at me properly. 'What are you doing here, May? And you're still in your nightdress. How the hell did you know something was wrong?'

'I told you, I —' I'm crying so much I can't say it.

'You didn't — *you* didn't do anything?' Rob whispers.

'Yes! I–I made an image of you out of dough and then I tried to stick nails in, but I couldn't so I burnt it and then I caused the fire.'

Rob stares at me — and then he starts laughing. He laughs so much that he has to let me go. He stands gasping, his eyes running with water, his hands flapping weakly. I don't like the way he laughs. It's too high-pitched and it sounds affected. His face is distorted, his eyes squeezed shut, his nostrils quivering, his mouth gaping, showing his fillings. Is he distorted — or am I seeing him clearly for the first time?

I find an old hankie in Auntie Win's jacket and I wipe my eyes. Auntie Win and Nan will be worried about me.

'I'd better go back.'

'I'll take you. I'll get a taxi. You can't walk home in your nightie and your bare feet. I can't believe you came all the way. And *how* did you know?'

'I told you.'

'You can't really believe in that sort of dotty magic.'

'It's not magic, it's witchcraft. It works. I know it does.'

209

'Of course it can't work,' says Rob and he puts his hands on my shoulders, steadying me. The people in the street are staring at us and I can feel myself blushing but Rob doesn't seem to care.

'All right, you made a model of me and stuck pins in it —'

'No, I told you, I put it in the boiler. I didn't mean it to burn like that though.'

'Anyway. You wanted to hurt me. Because I hurt you yesterday. I'm sorry about that. I was hateful. I thought it was all for the best.' His eyes flicker away and then he looks at me directly. 'No. Maybe I just panicked. Maybe there was a bit of truth in what you were saying and I didn't have the guts to take it. But that's not what I'm worrying about now. I'm worrying about you thinking you can do these witchcraft tricks. Can't you see, May, it was complete coincidence. And I bet you heard the fire engines. Only there wasn't a fire so you got it wrong, I didn't get burnt to a crisp.'

'It does work. There's been lots of things.'

'What things?'

'Well. The worse was ... my Grandad.' I'm crying again and Rob walks me along the road and sits me down on a garden wall, away from everyone. 'I painted this portrait of him, and then I blotted out his face ... and he died.'

'Oh May. He died because he was an old man. How could you seriously believe it was because you messed up a painting?'

'But I did it deliberately. I've worked the power of the shade.'

'What rubbish have you been reading? Look, I know some people think they're witches —'

'I'm a witch.'

'No you're not. You're a highly sensitive young girl with an over-developed imagination — God, don't I sound stuffy. But it's true. An old man dies and a gas stove explodes. That's not magic, May.'

'There were more things.'

210

'What?'

I can't tell him about Selina. I stare at the red heart on his sweater.

'It made you notice me,' I whisper.

'May.' His hands tighten on my shoulders. 'I'd have noticed you no matter what. Don't you realise that? You can work your own magic.'

# Chapter 26

The naked girl carefully balances a white wax mannikin, holding up a looking glass to make it reflect eerily in the moonlight. A wild man lurks nearby, his face contorted, his long sword skewering a dripping heart. An ancient hag holds up a swaddled child, its large head crammed into a dainty bonnet, its eyes unblinking as it watches the witches.

I watch the witches too. I stand and stare at the Salvator Rosa painting. People come and people go in the gallery but I stay standing and staring.

Am I a witch? Rob insists it's all nonsense. He asked me to stay behind after school — he still won't ask me back to his room — and he made me tell him all the spells and he laughed at them and made me laugh at them too. They did start to sound a little ridiculous sitting in the sunny classroom with Rob. I couldn't account for their shadowy power. I couldn't tell him about Selina. I won't betray her, even if we're not friends any more.

I don't know if Rob and I are true friends now. I stare at the red heart in the painting. Did the love charm really work? Did Rob ever love me? Did I ever love him? I don't think I love him now. He's laughed all the love away. And yet he takes my silly stories seriously enough. He's got them all properly typed out and he says he'd like to use them in his next book. I don't know whether I want him to use the stories. He changed them when he typed them out. He cut out bits and changed lots of the words. His words are better but the stories aren't mine any more. I think I'd like to write them out the old way and keep them for myself — but when I told Auntie Win Rob might use them she became excited.

'Of course you want to get them printed! Oh May, your stories in a real book that anyone could buy!'

'His book.'

'But he said he'll put your name in too.'

'I don't want him to use my name. I don't think I want to be in his book.' I hesitated. 'Maybe I could have my own book someday.'

Auntie Win didn't scoff. She took the idea seriously.

'Maybe you're not going to be an artist after all. Maybe you will be a writer,' she said. Then she sighed. 'Although you're so good at art, May. Almost as good as your mother.'

I looked at her and I wondered if I dared ask her: Are you Amy's mother? I shouted it inside my head but my lips didn't even twitch. I don't think I'll ever be able to ask her. And would she ever tell me if I did?

The baby in the picture could be a changeling child. Perhaps the old hag will care for her as best she can. The baby looks serious but it doesn't seem to be scared.

I'm scared of witchcraft. I'd be scared of these witches in the painting. They're not two girls giggling and playing games. They're adults and they're absorbed in their occult practices, steaming and manicuring a hanging corpse like demented beauticians, performing complicated rituals with sword and broomsticks and burning candles while the cauldron bubbles. They're not playing — one drink of that brew and you'd be dead.

I made the mannikin of Rob but I didn't seriously expect him to die. Or Bruno. Although I got so scared just in case I could make things happen. When you're really scared you'll believe anything.

I don't think Nan's gone senile either. I think she's simply too scared to accept Grandad's death. That's why she makes him up. She pretends he's in the next room or just down the road and then for a few minutes she can believe he might come back. She can't admit he's dead because that would put a stop to all her little games. The moment she admits he's really dead she's got to let all the sadness start, and she's never been very good at facing up to feelings. But maybe she had to hide her feelings in the past. What do you do if your husband starts sleeping with your sister and then she has his baby?

I try to imagine Grandad and Auntie Win in bed together but for once I can't make it work. I can't make them young enough and I can't take off their clothes. I can only go back as far as Amy's portrait, with Nan and Grandad on the sofa and Auntie Win in the chair. I can make Nan and Auntie Win change places easily enough, I can make Nan walk right out of the room, but when Grandad places his hand on Auntie Win's boney knee she blushes and bares her big teeth and Grandad's hand snaps back to his cardigan pocket as if it was on elastic.

No, he wouldn't be like that, not Grandad. He had such good gentle hands. They'd never fumble and probe. I blink hard to get that picture out of my head and the real Salvator Rosa painting blurs. When I get home I'm going to get out my painting of Grandad. I'm going to paint in his gentle smile and his soft white eyebrows and his milky blue eyes and then they'll be able to look at me for the rest of my life.

I know I couldn't ever have killed him.

'I love you, Grandad,' I whisper. 'I love you and I miss you and I'll always go on loving you and missing you.'

'Are you muttering your own incantations?'

I start and stare at the boy beside me. He's wearing an old blue collarless shirt, baggy striped trousers, a weird waistcoat with a watchchain, pink Argyle socks and plimsolls. It's a moment before I look at his face and then I go even redder.

'Hello May,' he says. 'I'm Bruno, remember? I used to go out with Selina.'

214

'How are you?' I ask urgently.

'I'm fine.'

'Good!'

'And were you?'

'What?'

'Making magic? The painting's called *Witches and their Incantations*.'

'Oh. I see. No!'

I stare back at the painting, willing my cheeks to whiten. I strain for something to say.

'Do you think Salvator Rosa was a witch too? Or did he hide and paint them secretly, without them knowing?'

'He didn't paint real witches. He just made them up.'

'Did he?'

'I think he'd seen some old woodcuts of witches and thought he'd have a go. The subject obviously appealed to him because he did a whole series of witch paintings.'

'And he made them all up?'

'As far as I know. Well, it wouldn't be real, would it? Look at all the weird beasties for a start.'

'Yes, but the witches themselves — I mean, people did practise witchcraft then, didn't they? Heaps of them got burnt for it. And — and some people still practise witchcraft today.'

'Oh dear, yes, I thought so. Selina's been working her little spells. What's she been doing? Sticking pins in a little model of me?' He sees my face and laughs.

'You don't think she really can work spells?'

'Of course not. And I don't think she believes it herself. It's just a way to make herself seem more interesting. I know her mother goes in for that sort of thing too. She's obviously influenced Selina. But I don't think she takes it that seriously either. I think it's all a big con.'

'That's what this friend of mine says.'

'Yes. Well. What have you been doing with yourself?'

I shrug. 'Things.'

'Are you still going to be an artist?'

'I think I want to write instead.'

'What sort of writing?'

'Maybe fairy stories.'

'Better than witches,' he says, glancing at the painting. He fishes in his waistcoat pocket for his watch.

'My Grandad had one just like that.'

'This was *my* Grandad's,' says Bruno. 'He used to let me play with his watch when I was a kid.'

'That's what I did too,' I say.

We both smile.

'Well, I've got to go. I'm meeting someone. See you around, May.'

Will he? Will we? I could make up my own incantation like the witches in the painting. But it wouldn't really work. It's all make believe. Figments of Salvator Rosa's imagination. Fragments of mine.

There was once a child who lived deep inside a mountain with a little tribe of trolls. They were very old and wizened and they looked fierce but they were kindly enough and they doted on the girl. She shivered in the cold cave so they plucked out their own thick hair and knitted it into warm woollen smocks and shawls to keep her cosy. She couldn't manage to scoop water in her hands from the underground stream so they carved her a goblet from a lump of emerald so she could sip in style. She was scared of the dark so they let her light one precious candle after another, although the storekeeper troll did sigh a little. She tossed and turned at night on the unyielding rock so they fashioned her a mattress out of moss. And when she still couldn't sleep they sang her lullabies.

They sang of the mountain and its secret caves of sapphires and emeralds. They sang of the maze of dark tunnels that circled them so safely. And they sometimes sang a lament about a girl who found her way along the dark tunnels and entered the outer world and was so sad she wept a river of tears and drowned in its depths. Tears trickled down the seamed cheeks of the trolls when they sang this song.

They sang jaunty marching chants when they set off to work each day. The girl begged to be taken to the innermost heart of the mountain so she could see the caves of precious stones for herself. It was such a long cold dark treck she was exhausted by the time she got there. The cave of emerald and the cave of sapphire did not seem very different from their own dwelling cave but she was a polite girl so she did her best to marvel.

She felt it was time she worked for her living so she borrowed a small pick and shovel and set to with a will. But her will soon wavered. Her thin arms ached as she swung them in the air. Her back hurt and her head throbbed. In half an hour her hands were badly blistered and she could scarcely draw breath. She had to lie flat on the floor to recover. The trolls laughed at her fondly. She was a pale and puny creature but they were sure she'd toughen up eventually. Her hands would harden, her back would stoop, her eyes would squint until she could see in the dark and stop fussing for a candle. She'd turn into a true troll given time.

But the girl didn't develop. She stayed soft and straight and she still hated the dark. She went a-mining every day but she couldn't get used to it. Her blisters bled and she ached in every bone. She could not stay polite under the circumstances. She grumbled and groaned and the trolls began to find her tiresome. They couldn't understand her at all.

'You'll never grow up to be a good troll if you don't pull yourself together,' they said.

'I don't want to be a silly old troll,' said the girl. 'I don't like it in this dark cold mountain. I want to go outside.'

The trolls trembled in distress.

'You must never say such things,' they hissed, and they covered her mouth with their calloused fingers.

The girl couldn't stop saying it. She couldn't stop thinking it. She begged the trolls to lead her out of the labyrinth so she could peep at the world from the entrance to the caves but they cowered at the thought.

'Remember the girl in the lament,' they said, and they sang it insistently night after night.

The words washed over the girl but they couldn't wash away her vision of the unknown outside world. It shone inside the dark of her head until she could see nothing else. She waited until the trolls were all asleep and snoring that night. She lit the longest candle she could find and set off down the narrow tunnel.

The treck to the outer mountain was much longer than the treck to the inner core. The tunnel twisted and turned, often so narrow she had to go down on her knees. The rock grew slimey under her bare feet and then a new underground stream surged up and soaked her. She waded through the water bravely, holding her candle high, out of harm's way. Then she reached a cave of bats and they swooped at the light and tangled themselves in her long hair like black bows. She combed them out frantically with

218

her fingers, trying to cling on to her candle, but there was a squeak and a smell of singeing wings and sudden darkness.

The girl screamed and the bats squeaked, mocking her. She brushed the air wildly and stumbled forward. And then she saw it. Far far away, at the very end of the tunnel. A tiny light. It didn't flicker like a candle. It was a steadfast glow.

The girl flicked the last bat from her curls and marched on towards the light. The tunnel widened and she walked faster and faster. The light grew larger. All the girl's senses stirred. She smelt fresh air for the first time. She heard faint birdsong. And she saw such a strange sight that her eyes widened until they watered. She saw blue. A blue much bluer than the biggest sapphire. A blue so beautiful it made her reel and she had to lean against the wall of the cave. Then she looked down and saw herself. She saw the whiteness of her own arm. She saw her hair falling over her shoulders, as red as flame. She saw the faded grey of her smock and shawl, made from the hair of the tired old trolls. She looked back once into the dark, but then she took a deep breath of the new air and walked out of the cave into the sunlight.

She stood there and she stared. The sight made her so dizzy she had to cling to the familiar rock with both hands — but even the rock felt strange. It was warm from the sun and little tufts of grass sprouted from its cracks and crannies. The girl was familiar with emerald and knew the colour green but she had never dreamt there could be so many subtle shades. She stared out over the hills and valleys, the woods and meadows, and she went white with wonder. She saw villages too and in the distance a town with a tall castle — but all the dwellings seemed equally awe-inspiring after a life lived in a cold cave. She felt the strange heat of the sun on her face and she rolled up the thick sleeves of her smock and stretched out her arms. This was her country. She could never go back to the dark core of the mountain.

She started making her way down the grassy slopes, slithering and sliding, running for the first time in her life. There was a river winding all the way round the mountain. All she had to do was cross over it and then she had left the mountain for ever.

But when she got to the river she saw it was much wider and much deeper than she realised. She held up her smock and tried wading but this was no underground stream. As soon as she was past the reeds at the edge of the bank the water rose rapidly. She felt its power rocking her off her feet. It seemed she would surely drown if she tried to cross this river. She clambered miserably back to the bank and lay there in her soaking clothes, close to despair. (But she did not cry. The river was deep enough already.) She hid her face in her hands nevertheless. And then a splash in the river made her look up. A beautiful silver fish glittered in the water, rising up on its tail so that it could address her with ease.

'Would you care to cross the river to the far bank?' it asked in such a sweet and silvery voice.

'Oh yes please, little fish,' said the girl.

'Then step into the shallows and sit on my silver scales. I will swim across the river with you.' The fish said it so sweetly — and yet

there was an odd gleam in its eye that made
the girl uneasy. But she desperately wanted
to cross the river so it seemed foolish not to
take a little chance. She stepped into the
shallows and climbed onto the slippery back
of the little fish.

'Off we go,' said the fish, and it started
swimming.

Just then the sun went behind a cloud and
when the girl looked down at the little fish
the silvery scales seemed much darker,
almost black. She shivered and the fish
suddenly dived downwards. The girl
screamed and slipped right off its back. The
water was black and the girl couldn't see,
couldn't swim. But in panic she struck out
wildly and by the greatest good fortune
managed to make it back to the bank. She
lay face down in the mud, clinging to the
reeds.

'What's the matter, little girl?'

She looked up and saw a black stallion
standing at the river bank, a magnificent
beast with a long dusky mane and tail.

'I want to cross the river but I don't know
how to do it,' she said, wiping her face with
her sodden shawl. 'A fish tried to swim me
across but it played a trick on me.'

'As if a little fish could help you,' said the
stallion. 'Climb on my back and I will leap
across the river right to the far bank.'

The girl climbed gratefully onto his back.
It seemed such a simple solution. But the
stallion wasn't quite so big as he had first
seemed. He galloped forwards but his legs
were small, almost stunted. The sun went
behind another cloud and the black stallion
looked almost grey, a smoky little pit pony.

'Stop, stop, we'll never make it!' the girl

221

shouted, and she slid from his back as he
gathered his strength to leap.

He did not even make it to the middle of
the river. He landed in the shallows,
stumbled about foolishly, and then trotted
lamely away.

The girl looked across the river. It was
such a long way. She didn't seem to have
much hope. There didn't seem to be any
other help at hand. She was left here all by
herself. So. She had herself.

She went down to the reeds. She plucked a
handful and cast them on the water. They
floated gracefully away. The girl watched
them carefully. Then she plucked up another
handful of reeds and another and another.
She didn't cast these away. She sat up on the
bank and started weaving. She had never
tried to weave before and at first she got into
a tangle, but after several attempts she sorted
the reeds and wound them in and out with
increasing dexterity. When she had made a
little mat of them she tried floating it on the
water — but it seemed very flimsy. She sat
and thought for a while and then she
scooped up some mud from the river bank
and ladled it evenly on both sides of the reed
mat. Then she let it bake in the hot sun.
While she waited for it to harden she hunted
around the river bank until she found a long
sappy stick, just right for a paddle. She felt
the muddy mat every now and then and
when it seemed hard she tried it on the water
once more. It bobbed up and down on the
ripples, a little raft. It still didn't look
particularly buoyant but it was the best she
could do.

She stepped on her reed raft and paddled
with her twig. The raft floated perfectly at

first and she paddled away proudly. But a little water oozed through the gaps in the reeds and the raft started tipping to one side. She crouched at the other end and kept paddling. Halfway across the twig caught in some rushes and broke so she had to lean right over and paddle with her hands. The raft tipped up on end and she fell into the water. She floundered about wildly and managed to grab a corner of the raft which she used as a float. She clutched it with both hands and kicked hard with her legs. She clutched and she kicked. It was not an elegant or easy way to travel but it got her there eventually. The sun was still shining when she stepped on to the far bank of the river.